Welcome to the World Heritage City of Bruges

There are places that somehow manage to get under your skin or work their way into your heart, even though you don't really know them all that well. Bruges is that kind of place. A warm and friendly place, a place made for people. A city whose history made it great, resulting in a well-deserved classification as a Unesco World Heritage site.

In this guide you will discover, experience and enjoy Bruges in all its many different facets. There are five separate chapters.

In **chapter 1**, you will learn everything you need to know to prepare for your visit to Bruges. There is a list of the ten 'must-see' sights, a brief summary of the city's rich past, a list of the best restaurants, useful tips for fun souvenirs and a mass of practical information, including details of the different options for getting around Bruges and a clear explanation about how best to use the 'Bruges City Card'. This card will allow you to visit many of Bruges' most important sites of interest for free or at a significantly reduced price.

The three inspiring walking routes included in **chapter 2** will take you to all the most beautiful spots in town. The detailed map of the city – which you can simply fold out of the back cover of this guide – will make sure that you don't lose your way. The map also shows the licensed places to stay in Bruges, offering a range of accommodation options that runs from charming guest rooms and holiday homes right through to star-rated hotels.

museums, sites of interest, and all its historic, cultural and religious buildings. Bruges' beautiful squares and enchanting canals are the regular backdrop for top-class cultural events. And few cities have such a rich and diverse variety of museums, which contain gems dating from the Flemish Primitives of medieval times to the finest modern art of today. Put simply, Bruges is always an experience – whether your interest is art, chocolate, diamonds or chips!

In Bruges you can dine at a different star-rated restaurant each day, or perhaps you would prefer lunch at a trendy bistro before wandering through the winding cobbled streets of the city? As far as food and drink is concerned, in Bruges you can find the best of all worlds. For centuries the local people have known all the best places to go. These are the places, full of charm and character, which you can read about in **chapter 4**. Five 'new arrivals' to the city will also tell you about their favourite places.

If you are staying a bit longer in the region, you may want to explore beyond the city boundaries. **Chapter 5** suggests a number of excursions to the Bruges Wet' and Woodland, the coast and the Westhoek.

The choice is yours!

Discover Bruges

The highlights of Bruge

The 10 classic places
that no one should miss!

Rozenhoedkaai:
a living picture postcard

The Rozenhoedkaai links the Belfry to the city's network of canals ('reien'). So perhaps it was inevitable that the quay should become one of the most photogenic locations in all of Bruges. In fact, this spot is so special that it is almost impossible not to take a photograph: a living postcard that you can be a part of!

A quiet moment in the Beguinage

Some places are so beautiful that you will have no choice but to feel awe. The Beguinage is such a beauty spot. When you amble through its quiet inner court, its purity will leave you speechless. Therefore take your time and while away along the romantic Minnewater, where you will fully enjoy the age-old view.
(Also see page 76)

Burg and City Hall: medieval opulence

The Burg is one of the city's most beautiful squares. For more than six centuries, Bruges has been governed from its 14th-century City Hall, one of the oldest and most venerable in the Low Countries. All this time this remarkable historic building has dominated this majestic square. Nowhere else will you be able to experience the city's wealth and affluence so strongly.

(Also see page 89)

The Flemish Primitives: world famous art from Bruges

Admire the unique and world-famous collection of pictures by the Flemish Primitives in the very city where they were painted. Or do you prefer the groundbreaking contemporary art scene, or perhaps poignant and romantic folklore or majestic town palaces? The Bruges Museums will happily serve all your needs.

(Also see pages 81-82, 87)

Wandering through the old Hansa Quarter

From the 13th to the 15th century, Bruges was an important trading centre at the crossroads between the Hansa cities of Scandinavia, England and Germany (known

collectively in those days as the 'Easterners') and the most important commercial regions in France, Spain and Italy. The Spanish traders established themselves at Spaanse Loskaai (Spanish Unloading Quay), while the Easterners set up shops on the Oosterlingenplein (Easterners' Square). Places where you can still sometimes feel the atmosphere of days long gone by.

The Canals of Bruges: the city's arteries

Experience the city by following an age-old tradition. Cruising Bruges' canals – the remarkable city arteries – you will discover secret gardens, picturesque bridges and wonderfully beautiful views. Although it sounds incredible, Bruges' loveliest places ooze even more charm when you admire them travelling by boat.

15 **31**

The Church of Our Lady: the centuries-old skyline of Bruges

The Church of Our Lady (Onze-Lieve-Vrouwekerk) is most remarkable for its 122 metre-high brick tower, a tribute to the skill of the city's medieval craftsmen and the second highest tower of its kind in the world. Inside the church you can wonder at the beauty of the *Madonna and Child*, a marble masterpiece sculpted by Michelangelo and guaranteed to leave no visitor unmoved.

(Also see page 85)

Almshouses: charity frozen in stone

Almshouses are tiny villages within the city's ramparts. That's how these medieval residential courts are best described. Centuries ago they were built out of mortar and charity. Today their picturesque gardens, whitewashed façades and glorious silence are the city's havens of peace par excellence.

(Also see page 46)

(14) Concert Hall or Culture with a capital C

This imposing and intriguing culture temple is a beacon of light and provides 't Zand, the square on which it stands, with a unique dynamic all on its own. Inside, there is no elaborate theatrical decoration, but a simple, almost minimalist, auditorium with a 'symphonic' arrangement of chairs. In short, the ideal circumstances in which to enjoy classical concerts, jazz, dance or theatre. *(More information on page 93)*

(04) (25)

Market Square – a must

If there is only one place you can visit in Bruges, this is it. The Market Square is literally and figuratively the beating heart of the city. The colourful guild houses, the clatter of horses' hooves, the rattling of the carriages and the dominating presence of the Belfry all combine to create a setting of great beauty and charm, which is part medieval and part modern. And if you are feeling energetic, you can still climb the 366 steps of the 83-metre high belfry tower, which will reward you with a spectacular panorama over the city and its surrounding hinterland. The Market is also the home of Historium, a brand-new top attraction that takes you back to the golden days of Bruges in the Middle Ages. The balcony on the first floor has a fine view of the square, with its statue of Jan Breydel and Pieter de Coninck, two of the city's most important historical figures. *(For more information about the Belfry see also pages 76-77 and for information about Historium see page 83)*

History in a nutshell

Water played a crucial role in the birth and development of Bruges.
It was at this place that a number of streams converged to form the
River Reie, which then flowed northwards towards the coastal
plain. Through a series of tidal creeks, the river eventually reached
the sea. Little wonder, then, that even as far back as Roman times
there was already considerable seafaring activity in this region.
This has been proven by the discovery of the remains of two
seagoing ships from this period, dating from the second half of
the 3rd century or the first half of the 4th century. Even so, it would
be another five centuries before the name 'Bruges' first began to
appear – the word being a derivative of the old-German word
'brugj', which means 'mooring place'. As the centuries passed,
Bruges developed into a commercial centre with its own port.

Its growing importance also resulted in it becoming the main fortified residence of the counts of Flanders, so that from the 11th century onwards the city was not only a prosperous trading metropolis, but also a seat of considerable political power.

Taking off

When the city's direct link with the sea was in danger of silting-up in the 12th century, Bruges went through a period of anxiety. Fortunately, the new waterway of the Zwin brought relief. As a result, Bruges was able to call itself the most important trade centre of Northwest Europe in the following century. The world's first stock exchange began business. Its financial exchanges took place on a square in front of the premises that belonged to Van der Beurse, a Bruges merchant family. In spite of the typical medieval maladies, from epidemics to political unrest and social inequality, the citizens of Bruges prospered, and soon the city developed a magnet-like radiation. Around 1350 the inner city numbered no fewer than 35.000 inhabitants.

Golden Age

Success continually increased. In the 15th century – Bruges' Golden Age – things improved further when the Royal House of Burgundy took up residence in the city. New luxury goods were produced in abundance, and famous painters such as Jan van Eyck and Hans Memling – the great Flemish Primitives – found their cre-

ative niche here. The fine arts flourished, and besides a substantial number of fine churches and unique merchant houses, a monumental town hall was also erected. Bruges' success seemed imperishable.

Decline

The death of the popular Mary of Burgundy in 1482 marked a sudden change of fortune. The relationship between the citizens of Bruges and their lord, the widower Maximilian, turned sour. The Burgundian court left the city, with the international traders following in its wake. Long centuries of wars and changes of political power took their toll. By the middle of the 19th century Bruges had become an impoverished city. Funnily enough, a novel would turn this wretched tide.

Revival

In *Bruges la Morte* (1892) Georges Rodenbach aptly describes Bruges as a somewhat sleepy, yet extremely mysterious place. Soon Bruges' magnificent patrimony was rediscovered and her mysterious intimacy turned out to be her greatest asset. Building on this élan, the city was provided with a new seaport, which was called Zeebrugge, whilst Bruges itself carefully took her first touristic steps. Success wasn't long in coming. UNESCO added the medieval city centre to its World Heritage list. The rest is history.

From early settlement to international trade centre (...-1200)

851   Earliest record of the city

863   Baldwin I takes up residence at Burg

1127   Charles the Good, Count of Flanders, is murdered in the Church of Saint Donatian; first town rampart; first Bruges city charter

1134   Creation of the Zwin that links Damme with the sea

Bruges' Golden Age (1369-1500)

1369   Margaret of Dampierre marries Philip the Bold, Duke of Burgundy. Beginning of the Burgundian period

1384   Margaret succeeds her father Louis of Male

1430   Marriage of Duke Philip the Good with Isabella of Portugal; establishment of the Order of the Golden Fleece

1436   Jan van Eyck paints the panel *Madonna with Canon Joris van der Paele*

1482   Margaret of Burgundy dies as a result of a fall from her horse

1488   Maximilian of Austria is locked up in Craenenburg House on Markt for a few weeks

851   **1200**   **1300**   **1500**

Bruges as the economic capital of Northwest Europe (1200-1400)

1245   Foundation of the Beguinage

1297   Second town rampart

1302   Bruges Matins and Battle of the Golden Spurs

1304   First Procession of the Holy Blood

1350   Reconstruction in stone of the Belfry after the destruction of its wooden predecessor

1376-1420   Construction of the City Hall

The city gets her second wind (1500-1578)

1506   The cloth merchant Jan Mouscron acquires Michelangelo's *Madonna and Child*

1528   Lancelot Blondeel designs the mantelpiece of the Liberty of Bruges

1548   Birth of the scientist Simon Stevin

1562   Marcus Gerards engraves the first printed town map of Bruges

1578   Bruges joins the rebellion against the Spanish king

An impoverished town in a pauperised Flanders (1584-1885)

- **1584** Bruges becomes reconciled with the Spanish king
- **1604** The Zwin is closed off
- **1713-1795** Austrian period
- **1717** Foundation of the Academy of Fine Arts, predecessor of the Groeninge Museum
- **1795-1814** French occupation
- **1799** Demolition of Saint Donatian's Cathedral and renovation of Burg
- **1815-1830** United Kingdom of the Netherlands
- **1830** Independence of Belgium; birth of the poet Guido Gezelle
- **1838** First railway station

The new city (1971-...)

- **1971** Amalgamation Law incorporates former suburbs
- **1985** King Baudouin opens new sea lock at Zeebrugge
- **2000** Historic city centre is given World Heritage status; Euro 2000 (European Football Championships)
- **2002** Cultural Capital of Europe
- **2008** *In Bruges* is released worldwide in cinemas
- **2010** The Procession of the Holy Blood is granted Intangible Cultural Heritage status by UNESCO

1600 **1700** **1800** **1900** **2000**

Provincial town with revived ambitions (1885-1970)

- **1887** Unveiling of the statue of Jan Breydel and Pieter de Coninck (Markt)
- **1892** Publication of *Bruges la Morte* by Georges Rodenbach
- **1896** Start of the construction of the seaport
- **1897** Dutch becomes the official language
- **1902** First exhibition of the Flemish Primitives
- **1914-1918** The Great War; Zeebrugge becomes a German naval base
- **1940-1945** The historic city centre survives Second World War almost unscathed
- **1958** First Pageant of the Golden Tree

Brugge City Card
Endless bargains

Would you like to explore Bruges and go easy on your wallet at the same time? Would you like to enjoy special offers whilst getting to know the city in all its aspects? With the Brugge City Card you will accumulate one discount after another and even visit countless museums and attractions completely free of charge. This super bargain card is handy, inexpensive and offers a unique chance to save more than € 250.00.

HOW DOES IT WORK?

Choose the validity period yourself: 48hrs or 72hrs. In the chapters *Exploring Bruges*, *Getting Around in Bruges* and *Excursions from Bruges* onwards, you will find a detailed overview of all museums, places of interest and attractions in and around Bruges. If you see a 🟦 then the Brugge City Card lets you in for free. If you see a 🟦 then you receive a hefty discount of at least 25% on the individual price. In addition, the free monthly magazine events@brugge handily lists all the events where the Brugge City Card offers you an extra discount.

The card will be automatically activated as soon as you use it for the first time. The card expires once the time limit has been exceeded. You can visit each attraction only once. Bear in mind that most museums are closed on Mondays.

These are our special offers

» Free entrance to 27 museums and places of interest in Bruges, including a hefty discount at the several museum shops to boot! Admire the world-famous paintings of the Flemish Primitives, gaze down onto the city from the top of the majestic Belfry and visit Choco-Story, the world's largest chocolate museum, or one of the other prestigious art collections.

» A free round trip on the canals (departures are only guaranteed in the period 1/3-14/11) or a city tour by minibus City Tour (only in the period 15/11-28/2). This is your chance to explore Bruges' secret nooks and crannies and its romantic hotspots.

» At least 25% discount on not to be missed concerts, dance and theatre performances.

» At least 25% discount on your bike rental.

» At least 25% discount at your underground car park.

» At least 25% discount at various museums, places of interest and attractions in the vicinity of Bruges.

» Only € 6.00 for a three-day pass of De Lijn, valid on all buses and trams in the whole of Flanders.

WHAT WILL IT COST YOU?

BRUGGE CITY CARD

48h € 40,00

72h € 45,00

HOW TO PLACE AN ORDER?

Call in at the information offices ℹ️ at the Markt (Historium), at 't Zand (Concertgebouw) or at the Stationsplein (Station, railway station), or order your City Card at www.bruggecitycard.be.

Museums and places of interest

▣	Archeologiemuseum (Archaeological Museum)	€4,00
▣	Arentshuis	€4,00
▣	Basiliek van het Heilig Bloed (Treasure chamber)	
	(Museum of the Basilica of the Holy Blood)	€2,00
▣	Begijnenhuisje (Beguine's house)	€2,00
▣	Belfort (Belfry)	€8,00
▣	Brouwerij (Brewery) De Halve Maan / guided tour + tasting	€7,50
▣	Choco-Story (Chocolate Museum)	€7,00
▣	Diamantmuseum Brugge (Bruges Diamond Museum)	
	+ diamond cutting demonstration	€9,50
▣	Expo Picasso	€8,00
▣	Frietmuseum (Belgian Fries Museum)	€6,00
▣	Gentpoort	€4,00
▣	Gezellemuseum (Gezelle Museum)	€4,00
▣	Groeningemuseum (Groeninge Museum) + visit to the Arentshuis	€8,00
▣	Gruuthusemuseum (Gruuthuse Museum)	€8,00
▣	Historium Bruges	€11,00
▣	Kantcentrum (Lace Centre)	€3,00
▣	Lumina Domestica (Lamp Museum)	€6,00
▣	Museum-Gallery Xpo Salvador Dalí	€10,00
▣	Onze-Lieve-Vrouwekerk (Church of Our Lady)	€6,00
▣	Onze-Lieve-Vrouw-ter-Potterie (Our Lady of the Pottery)	€4,00
▣	Sint-Janshospitaal (Saint John's Hospital) + pharmacy	€8,00
▣	Sint-Janshuismolen (Sint-Janshuis Mill) + Koeleweimolen (Koelewei Mill)	€3,00
▣	Sound Factory - Lantaarntoren	€6,00
▣	Stadhuis (City Hall) + Brugse Vrije (Liberty of Bruges)	€4,00
▣	Volkskundemuseum (Folklore Museum)	€4,00
▣	+ discount in the museum shops of the City Museums	-25%
▣	+ discount in the museum shop of the Bruges Diamond Museum	-10%

Culture and events

▣	Concertgebouw (Concert Hall)	-30%
▣	Cultuurcentrum Brugge (Cultural Centre)	-30%
▣	Kunstencentrum De Werf (Art Centre)	-25%

Gentpoort

Basilica of the Holy Blood

Saint John's Hospital

Concertgebouw

Museums around Bruges

Canada-Poland War Museum (Adegem)	€ 5,00 > € 4,00
Centrum Ronde van Vlaanderen (Tour of Flanders Centre, Oudenaarde)	€ 8,00 > € 6,00
In Flanders Fields Museum (Ypres)	€ 9,00 > € 6,50
Mu.ZEE (Ostend)	€ 5,00 > € 3,75
Mu.ZEE Ensorhuis (Ensorhouse, Ostend)	€ 2,00 > € 1,50
Mu.ZEE Permekemuseum (Permeke Museum, Jabbeke)	€ 3,00 > € 2,25
Museum Torhouts Aardewerk (Torhout Pottery Museum, Torhout)	€ 1,50 > € 1,00
Romeins Archeologisch Museum (Roman Archaeological Museum, Oudenburg)	€ 5,00 > € 3,00
Uilenspiegelmuseum (Damme)	€ 2,50 > € 1,50
Wijnendale Castle (Torhout)	€ 5,00 > € 3,00

Boat trip Lamme Goedzak (Bruges-Damme)

Port Cruise (Zeebrugge)

Boudewijn Seapark (Bruges)

Attractions around Bruges

🎫	Boudewijn Seapark (Bruges)	€ 25,00 > € 15,00
🎫	Seafront (Zeebrugge)	€ 12,50 > € 8,50

Sightseeing for next to nothing

🎫	Bruges on foot (only during the period 1/11-31/3)	€~~12,50~~
🎫	Bruges by boat	
	(departures are only guaranteed during the period 1/3 until 14/11)	€~~7,60~~
🎫	City Tour Bruges (minibus) (only during the period 15/11 until 28/2)	€~~16,00~~
🎫	Boat trip Lamme Goedzak (Bruges-Damme)	€ 10,50 > € 8,00
🎫	Port Cruise Zeebrugge	€ 9,50 > € 7,00
🎫	Bruges Ballooning	€ 170,00 > € 127,50

Transport

🎫	Parking Centrum-Zand/Centrum-Station/Pandreitje/Katelijne	- 25%
🎫	3-day pass of De Lijn*	€ 6,00
🎫	Electric Scooters (day rental)	class A: € 65,00 > € 48,75
		class B: € 75,00 > € 56,25

Bicycle rental points (day rental)

🎫	Bike rental Snuffel Backpacker Hostel	€ 8,00 > € 6,00
🎫	Bauhaus Bike Rental	€ 9,00 > € 6,00
🎫	B-Bike Concertgebouw	€ 12,00 > € 9,00
🎫	Fietsen 't Koffieboontje	€ 12,00 > € 9,00
🎫	Fietsen Popelier	€ 12,00 > € 9,00
🎫	Fietspunt (railway station)	€ 12,00 > € 9,00

* Only available at the information offices ℹ️ at the Markt (Historium),
at 't Zand (Concertgebouw) or at the Stationsplein (Station, railway station).

Exploring Bruges

You might want to stroll, amble and saunter down the streets of Bruges all day long or even for a whole weekend – nothing wrong with that. However, why not try to see the city from a different perspective? During a walking or bicycle tour, a guide will show you numerous secret places. Maybe you would prefer a boat trip on the mysterious canals – an unforgettable experience! And a ride in a horse-drawn carriage must surely be the perfect romantic outing. Sport-lovers can even do a guided run around the city. Or perhaps you simply want to tour all the highlights as quickly and as comfortably as possible? Then a minibus with expert commentary is what you need. And what about a balloon ride or a daytrip on a Vespa or an electric scooter? The choice is yours!

▥ ➤ Bruges by Boat

A visit to Bruges isn't complete without a boat trip on its canals. Go aboard at any of the five landing stages (consult city map) for a half-hour trip that allows you to appreciate the most noteworthy delights of the city from a completely different angle.

OPEN > March to mid November: daily 10.00 a.m.-6.00 p.m. (last departure at 5.30 p.m.)

PRICE > € 7.60; children aged 4 to 11 (accompanied by an adult): € 3.40; children under 4: free; Brugge City Card (during the period 1/3 until 14/11): free

Bruges on Foot

Not exhausted from walking around yet? Are you still in the mood for a guided tour? Then hurry to information office ▥ at 't Zand (Concertgebouw) and register for a two-hour fascinating guided walk. Languages: English, Dutch and French

▥ January/February/March/November/December: Monday, Wednesday and Saturday at 4.00 p.m. and Sunday at 10.30 a.m.

April: Saturday at 2.30 p.m. and Sunday at 10.30 a.m., but during the Easter holidays (5/4 until 20/4) also on working days at 2.30 p.m.

May/June/September/October: Saturday at 2.30 p.m. and Sunday at 10.30 a.m. July/August and during the period 5/4 until 20/4: Monday to Saturday at 2.30 p.m. and Sunday at 10.30 a.m. On 1/1 (New Year's Day), 20/4 (Easter Sunday), 21/4 (Easter Monday), 30/5 (the Friday after Ascension Day), 8/6 (Whit Sunday), 21/7 (National Holiday) 15/8 (Assumption of Mary) and 1/11 (All Saints' Day) at 10.30 a.m. There is no walk on 29/5 (Ascension Day).

PRICE > € 12.50; children under 12: free; Brugge City Card (during the period 1/11 until 31/3): free

INFORMATION & TICKETS > ▥ Information office at 't Zand (Concertgebouw) or www.ticketsbrugge.be

Photo Tour Brugge

Whether you are a photography expert or a photography novice, during the Photo Tour Andy McSweeney will take you to all the most photogenic spots in town! What are the 'must-have' shots for the photo report of your city trip to Bruges? You will learn this and lots more beside during a fascinating two-hour walk, complete with dozens of practical photography tips from Andy. The rendezvous point is the Basilica of the Holy Blood on the Burg Square. The walks are given in English, but Dutch and/or French can also be arranged on request.

OPEN > Four walks are organized each day, each with a different theme: 'Edges of Bruges' (at 10.00 a.m.) focuses on the side streets and canals; 'Essential Bruges' (1.00 p.m.) zooms in on the toppers; during 'Hidden Bruges' (4.00 p.m.) you will go in search of some of the city's less well-known corners and at 8.00 p.m. you can experience 'Bruges by Night'.

PRICE > € 40.00; children aged 10 years and under are free (if accompanied by an adult). Every paying participant receives five Bruges photos, specially taken by Andy McSweeney; every participating photographer can bring along one other non-photographer free of charge. Maximum of 5 photographers per walk. Prior reservation is recommended.

INFORMATION > Tel. +32 (0)486 17 52 75, info@phototourbrugge.com, www.phototourbrugge.com

Running around Bruges

Tourist Run Brugge – guided tours

Accompanied by a guide you run – at a gentle pace – through the streets and alleyways of Bruges. Because you either run early in the morning or early in the evening, you can freely admire Bruges. The circuit is 9.5 km long. With the expla-

nation that you receive along the way, you should allow 1 to 1.5 hours for completion. The start and finish are both on the Market Square, at the foot of the statue of Jan Breydel and Pieter de Coninck.

OPEN > On Friday, Saturday and the evenings before public holidays at 6.30 p.m.; on Wednesday, Sunday and public holidays at 8.00 a.m. and 6.30 p.m. Prior reservation is necessary.

PRICE > Including water, energy bar and city map with tips: € 15.00

INFORMATION > Tel. +32 (0)473 88 37 17, info@touristrunbrugge.be, www.touristrunbrugge.be

🐎 Bruges by Horse-drawn Carriage

The half-hour carriage ride along Bruges' historic winding streets trots off on Markt (at Burg on Wednesday morning). Halfway through the ride the carriage briefly stops at the Beguinage. The coachman gives expert commentary en route.

OPEN > Daily, 9.00 a.m.-6.00 p.m.; in July and August, 9.00 a.m.-10.00 p.m.

PRICE > € 39.00 per carriage; a carriage seats up to 5 people

INFORMATION > www.hippo.be/koets

Bruges by Hot Air Balloon

🚠 Bruges Ballooning

The most adventurous and probably the most romantic way to discover Bruges is by hot-air balloon. Bruges Ballooning organizes both a morning flight (including a champagne breakfast) and an evening flight (including a bite to eat, champagne or a beer) over Bruges. The whole trip lasts for three hours, with at least one hour in the air. You will be collected from wherever you are staying.

OPEN > During the period 1/4 until 31/10: daily flights, but only if booked in advance; bookings can be made on the day itself with a few hours notice, providing there are no prior reservations.

PRICE > € 170.00; children aged 4 to 12: € 110.00; Brugge City Card: € 127.50

INFORMATION > Tel. +32 (0)475 97 28 87, info@bruges-ballooning.com, www.bruges-ballooning.com

🚌 Bruges by bus

🚠 City Tour Bruges

The minibuses call at the different highlights of the city. They leave every 30 minutes from Markt for a fifty-minute trip. Headphones provide commentary in English, Dutch, French, German, Spanish, Italian and Japanese.

OPEN > The first bus leaves at 10.00 a.m. From March to October, the last bus leaves at 6.30 p.m. During the months of January, February, November and December the buses ride until sunset.

PRICE > Including audio guide: € 16.00; children aged 6 to 11: € 9.50; Brugge City Card (only during the period 15/11 until 28/2): free. A combi-ticket is possible *(see page 91)*.

INFORMATION > Tel. +32 (0)50 35 50 24 (Monday to Friday 10.00 a.m.-12.00 a.m), Info@citytour.be, www.citytour.be

Bruges by bike

QuasiMundo Biketours Bruges

• 'Bruges By Bike' > The narrow streets reveal the medieval character of the ancient port. The guide's fascinating stories will catapult you back to a time when knights and counts ruled the town. It goes without saying that there is a stop along the way for a thirst-quenching Belgian beer.

OPEN > During the period 1/3 until 15/11: daily, 10.00 a.m.-12.30 a.m.

• 'Border By Bike' > A tour through Bruges' wet- and woodlands, passing through medieval towns such as Damme,

peaceful Flemish agrarian villages and dead straight canals.

OPEN > During the period 1/3 until 15/11: daily, 1.00 p.m.-5.00 p.m.

Meeting Point: at the statue of *De Geliefden* (The Lovers) on Burg, ten minutes before departure of tour. English spoken. Booking is required.

PRICE > Including guide, raincoat, water and refreshment in a local café: € 28.00; youngsters (aged 8 to 26): € 26.00; children under 8: free. If you bring your own bike you get a reduction: adults: € 17.00; youngsters (8 to 26): € 16.00.

INFORMATION > Tel. +32 (0)50 33 07 75, info@quasimundo.eu, www.quasimundo.eu

The Pink Bear Bike Tours

A mere five minutes away from bustling Bruges lies one of the prettiest rural areas in Europe. You ride to historic Damme, the handsome medieval market town, once Bruges' outport. A guide will furthermore show you the most enchanting places of the Polders. It goes without saying that there is also a stop at a pleasant café for some Belgian Beers and/or Belgian waffles. On your return

you follow the beautiful poplar planted banks of a canal and discover some of Bruges' best-kept secrets.

Meeting Point: Belfry. English spoken.

OPEN > Daily: 10.25 a.m.-2.00 p.m. Booking is recommended; in January and February only possible with prior reservation.

PRICE > € 25.00; youngsters aged 9 to 26: € 23.00; children under 9: free; € 17.00 if you bring your own bike.

INFORMATION > Tel. +32 (0)50 61 66 86, www.pinkbear.freeservers.com

The Green Bike Tour/
The Sun Bike Tour

A guided trip to the polders, the flat countryside around Bruges. The tour pulls up at medieval Damme and other important sights along the way for a little extra commentary. Tandem rides can also be booked.

Meeting point: 't Zand, Concertgebouw. English, Dutch and French spoken. Booking is required.

OPEN > Daily, by appointment only

PRICE > € 15.00 (bike); € 30.00 (tandem); € 9.00 if you bring your own bike.

INFORMATION > Tel. +32 (0)50 61 26 67, arlando@telenet.be

Addresses of locations where you can hire bikes are given in the section Practical information *on page 32*

Bruges by scooter

📷 Electric Scooters

For those who want to explore Bruges quickly, silently and in ecologically-friendly motorized style (either by scooter or by electric bicycle)!

OPEN > During the period 1/4 until 30/9: Tuesday to Sunday, 10.00 a.m. - 6.00 p.m.; during the period 1/10 until 31/3: Tuesday to Friday, 2.00 p.m. - 6.00 p.m. and Saturday, 10.00 a.m. - 5.00 p.m.

PRICE > Including helmet and insurance: for an A-class scooter (max. speed 25 kph)> Emoto 87, for 2 persons: 2 hours: € 35.00; 8 hours: € 65.00 (with a Brugge City Card there is a reduction on the day price: € 48.75).
For a B-class scooter (max. speed 45 kph)> E-max 110S, for 2 persons: 2 hours: € 40.00; 8 hours: € 75.00 (with a Brugge City Card there is a reduction on the day price: € 56.25).

CONDITIONS > Minimum age of driver = 23 years; for a B-class scooter: A3 or B category driving license; deposit of € 100.00 to be paid before departure.

INFORMATION > Gentpoortstraat 62, tel. +32 (0)474 09 19 18, info@electric-scooters.be, www.electric-scooters.be

Vespa tours

Discover Bruges' wet- and woodlands in style: book a guided tour with a snazzy Vespa scooter and traverse the green polders, authentic villages and breath-taking landscapes. A couple of surprises are provided en route. Half-day and day

tours. You can also opt for the Cook & Drive a Vespa arrangement, a daylong programme with a fun mix of cooking and sightseeing. Booking is required. Meeting point: 't Zand. Dutch, French and English spoken.

OPEN > During the period 1/3 until 15/11: daily, 10.00 a.m.-6.00 p.m.

PRICE > Including helmet, experienced guide and insurance: half day tour: 1 person per Vespa: € 65.00; 2 persons per Vespa: € 80.00; day tour: 1 person per Vespa: € 100.00; 2 persons per Vespa: € 115.00.

CONDITIONS > Minimum age of driver: 21 years, driving licence B, deposit of € 200.00 to be paid before departure.

INFORMATION > Tel. +32 (0)497 64 86 48, bdpvespatours@gmail.com, www.vespatours-brugge.be

Award-winning restaurants

Bruges is called the epicentre of the world's gastronomy for good reason. The city places itself on the menu with an impressive list of first-class restaurants.

Michelin 2014   Source: Michelin Guide Belgium and Luxembourg 2014

» **De Karmeliet** ★★★   Chef Geert Van Hecke, Langestraat 19, 8000 Brugge, tel. +32 (0)50 33 82 59, www.dekarmeliet.be
» **Hertog Jan** ★★★   Chef Gert De Mangeleer, Torhoutse Steenweg 479, 8200 Sint-Michiels, tel. +32 (0)50 67 34 46, www.hertog-jan.com
» **De Jonkman** ★★   Chef Filip Claeys, Maalse Steenweg 438, 8310 Sint-Kruis, tel. +32 (0)50 36 07 67, www.dejonkman.be
» **A'Qi** ★   Chef Arnold Hanbuckers, Gistelse Steenweg 686, 8200 Sint-Andries, tel. +32 (0)50 30 05 99, www.restaurantaqi.be
» **Auberge De Herborist** ★   Chef Alex Hanbuckers, De Watermolen 15, 8200 Sint-Andries, tel. +32 (0)50 38 76 00, www.aubergedeherborist.be
» **Den Gouden Harynck** ★   Chef Philippe Serruys, Groeninge 25, 8000 Brugge, tel. +32 (0)50 33 76 37, www.goudenharynck.be
» **Sans Cravate** ★   Chef Henk Van Oudenhove, Langestraat 159, 8000 Brugge, tel. +32 (0)50 67 83 10, www.sanscravate.be

GaultMillau 2014   Source: GaultMillau, Belux 2014

» **Hertog Jan** (18,5/20)   Chef Gert De Mangeleer, Torhoutse Steenweg 479, 8200 Sint-Michiels, tel. +32 (0)50 67 34 46, www.hertog-jan.com
» **De Jonkman** (18/20)   Chef Filip Claeys, Maalse Steenweg 438, 8310 Sint-Kruis, tel. +32 (0)50 36 07 67, www.dejonkman.be
» **De Karmeliet** (18/20)   Chef Geert Van Hecke, Langestraat 19, 8000 Brugge, tel. +32 (0)50 33 82 59, www.dekarmeliet.be
» **A'Qi** (17/20)   Chef Arnold Hanbuckers, Gistelse Steenweg 686, 8200 Sint-Andries, tel. +32 (0)50 30 05 99, www.restaurantaqi.be
» **Den Gouden Harynck** (17/20)   Chef Philippe Serruys, Groeninge 25, 8000 Brugge, tel. +32 (0)50 33 76 37, www.goudenharynck.be

- » **Auberge De Herborist** (16/20) Chef Alex Hanbuckers, De Watermolen 15, 8200 Sint-Andries, tel. +32 (0)50 38 76 00, www.aubergedeherborist.be
- » **Sans Cravate** (16/20) Chef Henk Van Oudenhove, Langestraat 159, 8000 Brugge, tel. +32 (0)50 67 83 10, www.sanscravate.be
- » **Zeno** (16/20) Chef Reinout Reniere, Vlamingstraat 53, 8000 Brugge, tel. +32 (0)50 68 09 93, www.restaurantzeno.be
- » **Patrick Devos** (15/20) Chef Patrick Devos, Zilverstraat 41, 8000 Brugge, tel. +32 (0)50 33 55 66, www.patrickdevos.be
- » **Tanuki** (15/20) Chef Ivan Verhelle, Oude Gentweg 1, 8000 Brugge, tel. +32 (0)50 34 75 12, www.tanuki.be
- » **Bistro Refter** (14/20) Chef Frederiek Hoorne, Molenmeers 2, 8000 Brugge, tel. +32 (0)50 44 49 00, www.bistrorefter.be
- » **Bonte B** (14/20) Chef Bernard Bonte, Dweersstraat 12, 8000 Brugge, tel. +32 (0)50 34 83 43, www.restaurantbonteb.be
- » **Bruut** (14/20) Chef Bruno Timperman, Meestraat 9, 8000 Brugge, tel. +32 (0)50 69 55 09, www.bistrobruut.be
- » **Goffin** (14/20) Chef Timothy Goffin, Maalse Steenweg 2, 8310 Sint-Kruis, tel. +32 (0)50 68 77 88, www.timothygoffin.be
- » **Le Manoir Quatre Saisons** (14/20) Chef Olivier Christiaens, Heilige-Geeststraat 1, 8000 Brugge, tel. +32 (0)50 34 30 01, www.castillion.be
- » **'t Pandreitje** (14/20) Chef Guy Van Neste, Pandreitje 6, 8000 Brugge, tel. +32 (0)50 33 11 90, www.pandreitje.be
- » **Rock Fort** (14/20) Chef Hermes Vanliefde, Langestraat 15, 8000 Brugge, tel. +32 (0)50 33 41 13, www.rock-fort.be
- » **Assiette Blanche** (13/20) Chef Stefaan Timmerman, Philipstockstraat 23-25, 8000 Brugge, tel. +32 (0)50 34 00 94, www.assietteblanche.be
- » **Bhavani** (13/20) Chef Guy Suresh Acharya, Simon Stevinplein 5, 8000 Brugge, tel. +32 (0)50 33 90 25, www.bhavani.be
- » **Burg 9** (13/20) Chef Kristof De Kroon, Burg 9, 8000 Brugge, tel. +32 (0)50 33 35 99, www.burg9.be
- » **Den Dyver** (13/20) Chef Achim Vandenbussche, Dijver 5, 8000 Brugge, tel. +32 (0)50 33 60 69, www.dyver.be
- » **Kardinaalshof** (13/20) Sint-Salvatorskerkhof 14, 8000 Brugge, tel. +32 (0)50 34 16 91, www.kardinaalshof.be
- » **Lieven** (13/20) Chef Lieven Vynck, Philipstockstraat 45, 8000 Brugge, tel. +32 (0)50 68 09 75, www.etenbijlieven.be
- » **La Tâche** (13/20) Chef Olivier Monbailliu, Blankenbergse Steenweg 1, 8000 Sint-Pieters, tel. +32 (0)50 68 02 52, www.latache.be
- » **Tête Pressée** (13/20) Chef Pieter Lonneville, Koningin Astridlaan 100, 8200 Sint-Michiels, tel. +32 (0)470 21 26 27, www.tetepressee.be

» **De Visscherie** (13/20)   Chef Björn Verriest, Vismarkt 8, 8000 Brugge,
tel. +32 (0)50 33 02 12, www.visscherie.be

» **Weinebrugge** (13/20)   Chef Benny De Bruyn, Leikendreef 1, 8200 Sint-Michiels,
tel. +32 (0)50 38 44 40, www.weinebrugge.be

» **'t Zwaantje** (13/20)   Chef Geert Vanhee, Gentpoortvest 70, 8000 Brugge,
tel. +32 (0)473 71 25 80, www.hetzwaantje.be

» **Channel 16** (👍)   Werfkaai 16, 8380 Zeebrugge, tel. +32 (0)50 60 16 16, www.ch16.be

» **Duc de Bourgogne** (👍)   Huidenvettersplein 12, 8000 Brugge,
tel. +32 (0)50 33 20 38, www.ducdebourgogne.be

» **De Florentijnen** (👍)   Academiestraat 1, 8000 Brugge, tel. +32 (0)50 67 75 33,
www.deflorentijnen.be

» **Huyze Die Maene** (👍)   Markt 17, 8000 Brugge, tel. +32 (0)50 33 39 59,
www.huyzediemaene.be

» **'t Jong Gerecht** (👍)   Langestraat 119, 8000 Brugge, tel. +32 (0)50 31 32 32,
www.tjonggerecht.be

» **Kwizien Divien** (👍)   Hallestraat 4, 8000 Brugge, tel. +32 (0)50 34 71 29,
www.kwiziendivien.be

» **De Mangerie** (👍)   Oude Burg 20, 8000 Brugge, tel. +32 (0)50 33 93 36,
www.mangerie.com

» **Parkrestaurant** (👍)   Minderbroedersstraat 1, 8000 Brugge, tel. +32 (0)497 80 18 72,
www.parkrestaurant.be

Bib Gourmand 2014   Source: Bib Gourmand Benelux 2014

» **Assiette Blanche**   Chef Stefaan Timmerman, Philipstockstraat 23-25,
8000 Brugge, tel. +32 (0)50 34 00 94, www.assietteblanche.be

» **'t Apertje**   Chef Leo Callewaert, Damse Vaart-Zuid 223, 8310 Sint-Kruis,
tel. +32 (0)50 35 00 12, www.apertje.be

» **Bistro Kok au Vin**   Chef Jürgen Aerts, Ezelstraat 21, 8000 Brugge,
tel. +32 (0)50 33 95 21, www.kok-au-vin.be

» **Bistro Refter**   Chef Frederiek Hoorne, Molenmeers 2, 8000 Brugge,
tel. +32 (0)50 44 49 00, www.bistrorefter.be

» **Channel 16**   Chef Christian Van den Ouden, Werfkaai 16, 8380 Zeebrugge,
tel. +32 (0)50 60 16 16, www.ch16.be

» **Kurt's Pan**   Chef Kurt Van Daele, Sint-Jakobsstraat 58, 8000 Brugge,
tel. +32 (0)50 34 12 24, www.kurtspan.be

» **Restaurant Pergola**   Hotel Die Swaene, Meestraat 7, 8000 Brugge,
tel. +32 (0)50 44 76 50, www.restaurantpergola.be

» **Tête Pressée**   Chef Pieter Lonneville, Koningin Astridlaan 100, 8200 Sint-Michiels,
tel. +32 (0)470 21 26 27, www.tetepressee.be

Overnight stays in Bruges

Whether you opt for a classy four-star hotel, a charming B&B, a cheap-and-cheerful youth hostel or an authentic holiday home, one thing is certain: in Bruges there is always plenty of choice and you will always spend the night in style.

On the reverse side of the handy city plan – which you can remove from the back of this guide – you will find a list of licensed accommodation options, grouped by type. There are also useful directions for how to get to each li-cenced accommodation address – not only for people travelling by car, but also for users of public transport.

Accommodation reservations can be made online via www.brugge.be or directly with the outlet of your choice.

Souvenirs from Bruges

There is nothing more pitiful than returning home with a trivial souvenir that is immediately exiled to a cupboard – Bruges offers a solution. The World Heritage City impresses with a selection of authentic gadgets, novelties and other objects that you would dearly love to keep for yourself. From unique lacework and glittering diamonds to foamy local beers and irresistibly delicious chocolate. Too good and too tempting to resist!

Because Bruges is easily accessible and because the main shopping streets are close to each other, a 'day at the shops' in the city's old historic centre is a pleasant and carefree experience. As well as the better-known chain stores, there is a wide range of smaller shops and boutiques. And for those who are prepared to step off the beaten track, there are always exciting discoveries to be made.

The most important shopping streets run from the Markt (Market Square) to the old city gates (the shopping area is coloured in yellow on the street plan). Hidden away between Noordzandstraat and Zuidzandstraat there is a small but interesting shopping centre: Zilverpand. Each neighbourhood has its own character. In the main shopping streets you will find the famous brands and names, while (for example) the Langestraat is full of second-hand stores and interesting shops.

Lace

You don't fancy a boring, run-of-the-mill souvenir? Why not purchase some unique Bruges lace? A fine piece of fancywork with an incontestable reputation, Bruges and its lace have been inextricably bound up with one another

Lace through the centuries

The story of lace in Bruges began in the 16th century. It soon played an important role in the artistic, economic and social life of the city. The craft was a protected one and the religious orders quickly developed it into a veritable industry. In the lace schools, young girls – often from poor families – learnt lace-making skills, whilst at the same time being kept 'on the right path' by the guardians of the church! After 1850, lace became a domestic industry. Housewives made pieces of lace at home, which were then bought up for next-to-nothing by go-betweens, who then sold them for a huge profit. During the second half of the 19th century more than 10,000 women were employed in Bruges in this manner. The level of exploitation was disgraceful: most lace workers earned scarcely half the average wage of the day. After the First World War the demand for handmade lace fell dramatically and today it has almost disappeared as a viable economic activity. Fortunately, the lace-making skills have been passed down in Bruges from generation to generation and are still well known in the city today. Did you know that the Bruges Lace School developed a simple method for learning the techniques of bobbin lace-making, which is now taught all over the world? The different techniques are linked to colours: simple and easy to follow in any language! Various training courses are still organized in the Bruges Lace Centre, teaching the tricks of the trade to lace enthusiasts from far and wide.

More info on www.kantcentrum.eu

since time immemorial. Thousands of female hands have brought Bruges lace its deserved worldwide fame, and it also provided countless girls and women with a welcome addition to their income. Once half of the female population of Bruges was making bobbin lace. Today you can still see lacemakers at work here and there. It is such fun to try and follow their dexterity with their fingers. Or would you prefer an attempt at bobbin lacing yourself? At the Lace Centre, experienced lacemakers will teach you the tricks of the trade. See page 84 for all practical information.

Beer

Let's not beat about the bush. A Brugean enjoys a pint of beer now and then, especially if the beer has been brewed in his own city. So it is logical that Bruges boasts no fewer than two local beers: 'Straffe Hendrik' and 'Brugse Zot', brewed by the De Halve Maan Brewery. You won't find many beers like this. In short, they are internationally acclaimed success stories that taste of more, beers so full of character that you will definitely want to take them home with you in order to share them with the rest of the world. After all, it would be a shame to let only the citizens of Bruges smack their lips, wouldn't it? Convinced? Then return to the annual Bruges Beer Festival and discover even more hidden treasures! You can read more about Bruges Beer Festival on page 94 and about the De Halve Maan Brewery on pages 77-78.

Diamonds

In the 14th century Bruges was already the centre of a thriving diamond industry.

Diamonds were expertly cut here. This is really no surprise, because diamond cutting on a revolving disc was invented by the local goldsmith Lodewijk van Berquem in 1476. A year later the emperor Maximilian of Austria offered Mary of Burgundy the very first diamond engagement ring in history. It is obvious the Dukes of Burgundy valued beauty very much. At the Diamond lab of the Bruges Diamond Museum you will be able to find some sparkling inspiration, and you will also learn how to assess all this brilliance. You will then be able to use your expert eye at the museum shop or the countless jeweller's in town before you seize your opportunity. See pages 79-80 for detailed information about Bruges Diamond Museum.

Chocolate

A serious chocolate guild, the 'Brugsch Swaentje' (Bruges' Swan): the city's own delicious chocolate, a fascinating chocolate museum and even a scrumptious chocolate walk. What an abundance of quality guarantees, wouldn't you say? It only stands to reason that Bruges calls itself the chocolate capital of the world. In other words, if you don't succumb to a piece of chocolate here, you will never do so. Almost the entire city is covered in the sweet smell of this delicacy, as around every corner a chocolate temptation is lurking. Bruges counts more than fifty excellent chocolate shops, providing the visitor with whatever they're looking for, from exquisite old-fashioned solidity and delectable trinkets for individual use to ingenious molecular chocolate hocus-pocus cooked up by Michelin starred chefs. You can discover more about chocolate on pages 78-79.

Practical information

Bicycle rental points

🚲 Fietspunt Station
LOCATION > Hendrik Brugmansstraat 3
(Stationsplein, Railway station Square)
PRICE > 1 hour: € 4.00; 4 hours: € 8.00; full day:
€ 12.00 (Brugge City Card: € 9.00)
OPENING TIMES > Monday to Friday, 7.00
a.m-7.30 p.m.; during the periode 1/4 until
15/11: also during weekends and on holidays,
9.00 a.m.-9.40 p.m.
INFORMATION > Tel. +32 (0)50 39 68 26

🚲 De Ketting
LOCATION > Gentpoortstraat 23
PRICE > € 6.00/day. Price electric bike:
€ 20,00/day
OPENING TIMES > During the period 15/4 until
15/10: daily, 10.00 a.m.-12.15 a.m and 1.15 p.m.-
6.30 p.m.; during the period 16/10 until 14/04:
Monday, 1.30 p.m.-6.30 p.m., Tuesday to Saturday, 10.00 a.m.-12.15 a.m and 1.30 p.m.-6.30 p.m
INFORMATION > Tel. +32 (0)50 34 41 96,
www.deketting.be

🚲 Eric Popelier
LOCATION > Mariastraat 26
PRICE > 1 hour: € 4.00; 4 hours: € 8.00; full day:
€ 12.00 (Brugge City Card: € 9.00). Price electric bike 1 hour: € 10.00; 4 hours: € 17.00; full
day: € 30.00. Price tandem 1 hour: € 10.00;
4 hours: € 17.00; full day: € 25.00. Price reduction for students
OPENING TIMES > During the period 1/3 until
31/10: daily, 10.00 a.m.-7.00 p.m.; during the
period 1/11 until 28/2: Tuesday-Sunday, 10.00
a.m.-6.00 p.m.
INFORMATION > Tel. +32 (0)50 34 32 62,
www.fietsenpopelier.be

🚲 't Koffieboontje
LOCATION > Hallestraat 4
PRICE > 1 hour: € 4.00; 4 hours: € 8.00; full day:
€ 12.00 (Brugge City Card: € 9.00); students (on display of a valid student card): € 9.00. Price tandem
1 hour: € 10.00; 4 hours: € 18.00; full day: € 25.00
OPENING TIMES > Daily, 9.00 a.m.-10.00 p.m.
INFORMATION > Tel. +32 (0)50 33 80 27,
www.bikerentalbruges.be

🚲 Bauhaus Bike Rental
LOCATION > Langestraat 145

PRICE > 3 hours: € 6.00; full day: € 9.00 and
during the period 1/10 until 31/3: € 6.00
(Brugge City Card: € 6.00)
OPENING TIMES > During the period 1/4
until 30/9, 9.00 a.m.-9.00 p.m. (bikes must be
returned by 9.00 p.m.); during the period
1/10 until 31/3, 10.00 a.m-6.00 p.m.
INFORMATION > Tel. +32 (0)50 34 10 93,
www.bauhaus.be/services/bike-rental

🚲 Snuffel Backpacker Hostel
LOCATION > Ezelstraat 47-49
PRICE > Full day: € 8.00 (Brugge City Card: € 6.00)
OPENING TIMES > Daily, 8.00 a.m.-8.00 p.m.
INFORMATION > Tel. +32 (0)50 33 31 33,
www.snuffel.be

🚲 B-Bike Concertgebouw
LOCATION > 't Zand
PRICE > 1 hour: € 4.00; 4 hours: € 8.00; full day:
€ 12.00 (Brugge City Card: € 9.00)
OPENING TIMES > During the period 1/4
until 15/10: daily, 10.00 a.m.- 7.00 p.m; during
the period 16/10 until 31/3: weekends only
10.00 a.m.-12.00 a.m. and 1.00 p.m.-7.00 p.m.
INFORMATION > Tel. +32 (0)479 97 12 80

🚲 Bruges Bike Rental
LOCATION > Niklaas Desparsstraat 17
PRICE > 1 hour: € 3.50; 2 hours: € 5.00; 4 hours:
€ 7.00; full day: € 10.00; students (on display
of a valid student card): € 8.00. Price tandem
1 hour: € 8.00; 2 hours: € 12.00; 4 hours: € 15.00;
full day: € 20.00; students (on display of a valid student card): € 17.00
OPENING TIMES > Daily: 10.00 a.m.-8.00 p.m.
INFORMATION > Tel. +32 (0)50 61 61 08,
www.brugesbikerental.be

🚲 Electric Scooters
Hire of electric bikes.
LOCATION > Gentpoortstraat 55 and 62
PRICE > 2 hours: € 10.00; 4 hours: € 18.00 and
8 hours: € 30.00
OPENING TIMES > During the period 1/4
until 30/9: Tuesday-Sunday, 10.00 a.m.-
6.00 p.m.; during the period 1/10 until 31/3:
Tuesday-Friday, 2.00 p.m.- 6.00 p.m. and
Saturday, 10.00 a.m.- 5.00 p.m.
EXTRA > Electric scooters (see page 23)
INFORMATION > Tel. +32 (0)474 09 19 18,

info@electric-scooters.be,
www.electric-scooters.be

Most of the bicycle rental points ask for the payment of a guarantee.

Camping cars

The Kanaaleiland (Canal Island) in the Bargeweg offers an excellent all-year-round parking area for camping cars. Once your camper is parked, you are just a five-minute walk from the city centre (via the Beguinage). The parking area is open for new arrivals until 10.00 p.m. It is not possible to make prior reservations.
PRICE > During the period 1/3 until 30/9: € 22.50/day; during the period 1/10 until 28/2: € 15.00/day. Electricity is free, there are bins for selective waste disposal, and also the possibility to discharge dirty water and take on a new supply of clean water.

Church services

01 **Basiliek van het Heilig Bloed (Basilica of the Holy Blood)**
daily (except Thursday): 11.00 a.m.

02 **Begijnhofkerk (Beguinage)**
Monday-Saturday: 7.15 a.m., Sunday: 9.30 a.m.

12 **English Church**
(Saint Peter's Chapel)
English language service, Anglican
Sunday: 6.00 p.m.

06 **Heilige Familiekerk (Holy Family)**
Saturday: 5.30 p.m.

07 **Heilige Magdalenakerk (Holy Magdalene)**
Sunday: 11.30 a.m.

09 **Jezuïetenhuis (Jesuits)**
Monday-Friday: 12.00 a.m.,
Saturday: 17.00 p.m., Sunday: 11.30 a.m.

10 **Kapucijnenkerk (Capuchins)**
Monday-Friday 8.00 a.m., Saturday 6.00 p.m.,
Sunday 7.00 a.m. and 10.30 a.m.

11 **Karmelietenkerk (Carmelites)**
Monday-Friday 7.00 a.m., Saturday: 6.00 p.m.,
Sunday: 10.00 a.m.

15 **Onze-Lieve-Vrouwekerk (Church of Our Lady)**
Tuesday and Thursday: 9.00 a.m.,
Saturday: 5.30 p.m., Sunday: 11.00 a.m.

16 **Onze-Lieve-Vrouw-ter-Potteriekerk (Our Lady of the Pottery)**
Monday-Friday: 6.45 a.m.,
Sunday: 7.00 a.m. and 9.30 a.m.

17 **Onze-Lieve-Vrouw-van-Blindekenskapel (Our Lady of the Blind)**
Saturday: 6.00 p.m.

18 **Orthodoxe Kerk HH. Konstantijn & Helena (Orthodox Church Saints Constantin & Helen)**
Saturday: 6.00 p.m., Sunday: 9.00 a.m.

19 **Sint-Annakerk (Saint Anne)**
Sunday: 10.00 a.m.

20 **Sint-Gilliskerk (Saint Giles)**
Sunday: 7.00 p.m.

21 **Sint-Godelieveabdij (Saint Godelina's Abbey)**
Monday Saturday: 8.25 a.m.,
Sunday: 9.30 a.m.

22 **Sint-Jakobskerk (Saint Jacob)**
Saturday: 6.30 p.m.

23 **Sint-Salvatorskathedraal (Saint Saviour)**
Monday-Friday 6.00 p.m.,
Saturday 4.00 p.m., Sunday 10.30 a.m.

12 **Verenigde Protestantse Kerk (United Protestant Church)**
('t Keerske)
Sunday: 10.00 a.m.

25 **Vrije Evangelische Kerk (Free Evangelical Church)**
Sunday: 10.00 a.m.

Cinemas

» All films are shown in their original language.

08 **Cinema Liberty**
Kuipersstraat 23, www.cinema-liberty.be

09 **Cinema Lumière**
Sint-Jakobsstraat 36, www.lumiere.be

10 **Kinepolis Brugge**
Koning Albert I-laan 200, Sint-Michiels,
www.kinepolis.com | bus: no. 27, stop:
Kinepolis

Climate

Bruges enjoys a mild, maritime climate. The
summers are warm without being hot and the
winters are cold without being freezing. During spring and autumn the temperatures are
also pleasant and there is moderate rainfall
throughout the year, with the heaviest con-
centrations in autumn and winter. So remember to bring your umbrella!

Emergencies

► **European emergency number**

» Tel. 112. This general number is used in all
countries of the European Union to contact
the emergency services: police, fire brigade
or medical assistance. The number operates
24 hours a day, 7 days a week.

► **Medical help**

» **Doctors on duty**
7.00 p.m.-8.00 a.m. > tel. +32 (0)78 15 15 90
» **Pharmacists on duty**
tel. +32 (0)900 10 500
» **Dentists on duty**   tel. +32 (0)903 39 969
» **S.O.S. Emergency Service**   tel. 100
» **Hospitals**
A.Z. St.-Jan > tel. +32 (0)50 45 21 11
A.Z. St.-Lucas > tel. +32 (0)50 36 91 11
St.-Franciscus Xaveriuskliniek >
tel. +32 (0)50 47 04 70
» **Poisons Advice Centre**
tel. +32 (0)70 245 245

► **Police**

» **General telephone number**
tel. +32 (0)50 44 88 44
» **Emergency police assistance**   tel. 101
» **Working hours**
Monday-Saturday: 8.00 a.m.- 6.00 p.m. you
can contact the central police services at
Kartuizerinnenstraat 4 | city map: E9
» **After working hours**
There is a 24/24 permanence at the police
station at the Lodewijk Coiseaukaai 3 |
city map: F1

Formalities

» **Identity**
An identity card or valid passport is necessary.
Citizens of the European Union do not require
an entrance visa. If you arrive in Belgium from
outside the European Union, you must first
pass through customs. There are no border
controls once inside the European Union.

» **Health**
Citizens of the European Union can use their
own national health insurance card/docu-
ment to obtain free medical treatment in
Belgium. You can obtain this card from your
own national health service. Please note,
however, that every member of the family
must have his/her own card/document.

Getting there

► **By train**

» London (Saint Pancras) – Bruges by Euro-
star in 3.20 hours, one transfer in Brussels
(station Midi/Zuid).
» Also one transfer at Brussels (Midi/Zuid)
when coming from other European cities like
Amsterdam, Paris, Rotterdam, Cologne and
Luxembourg. Multiple direct connections
each day from Brussels, Ghent and Antwerp,
but also from other Belgian cities to Bruges.

► **By car / coach / ferry**

» Dover (UK) – Dunkirk (F) with DFDS Seaways |
Dunkirk (F) > Bruges (B) by car: 45 miles /
50 minutes.
» Dover (UK) – Calais (F) with DFDS Seaways
or P&O ferries | Calais (F) > Bruges by car:
72 miles / 80 minutes.
» Hull (UK) – Zeebrugge (B) with P&O ferries |
Zeebrugge > Bruges by car: 10 miles /
20 minutes.

Please note!   Maximum speed limit in the
city centre is 30 km/h.

► **By plane**

» **Via Brussels Airport**
Daily flights from 200 destinations in 66 countries. Easy access to Bruges by train (one
transfer in Brussels-Midi/Zuid).
» **Via Brussels-South-Charleroi-Airport**
Multiple flights a week with low-cost airlines
from several European cities. There is a regular train connection between Brussels-South
airport and Midi/-Zuid railway station.
Frequent train connections between

► How to get to Bruges?

Departure	via	km	mls	time train 🕑	time boat 🕑	Make a reservation
Amsterdam	Antwerp	253	157	3:05	-	www.b-europe.be
Cologne (Köln)	Brussels Midi/Zuid	313	194	3:13	-	www.bahn.de
London St Pancras	Brussels Midi/Zuid	-	-	3:20	-	www.eurostar.com
Lille Flandres	Kortrijk	75	47	1:19	-	www.b-europe.be
Paris Nord	Brussels Midi/Zuid	296	184	2:36	-	www.thalys.com
Brussels Airport	Brussels North or Midi/Zuid	110	68	1:25	-	www.b-rail.be
Hull	Zeebrugge	-	-	-	1 night	www.poferries.com
Dover	Dunkerque	-	-	-	2:00	www.dfds.com
Dover	Calais	-	-	-	1:30	www.poferries.com
Dover	Calais	-	-	-	1:30	www.dfds.com
Dover	Calais	-	-	-	1:30	www.myferrylink.com

Brussels Midi/Zuid and Bruges.
More information on www.brugge.be

Good to know

With its wide shopping streets, inviting terraces, trendy eating houses and stylish hotels, Bruges is a paradise for shoppers. But don't let your shopping pleasure be ruined by pickpockets. Always keep your wallet/purse in a closed inside pocket, and not in an open handbag or rucksack. Remember – thieves like shopping too!
Bruges is a lively, fun-loving city, with great nightlife. There are plenty of places where you can amuse yourself until the early hours of the morning. Please bear in mind that it is forbidden to sell strong drink (15% or more) to people under 18 years of age. For people under 16 years of age, this prohibition also applies to beer and wine (all drinks with an alcoholic content in excess of 0.5%).
Visiting Bruges means endless hours of fun, but please allow the visitors who come after you to enjoy their fun in a clean and tidy city: so always put your rubbish in a rubbish bin.

ℹ️ Info offices

There are three tourist information offices in Bruges: one in the Historium (Market Square), one in the Concertgebouw (Concert Hall) and a third in the railway station.
» **Info office Markt (Historium)**
Markt 1
Daily: 10.00 a.m.-5.00 p.m.

» **Info office 't Zand**
(Concertgebouw, Concert Hall)
't Zand
Monday-Saturday: 10.00 a.m.-5.00 p.m.
Sunday and public holidays: 10.00 a.m.-2.00 p.m.
» **Info office Stationsplein**
(Station, railway station)
Stationsplein
Monday-Friday: 10.00 a.m.-5.00 p.m.
Saturday and Sunday: 10.00 a.m.-2.00 p.m.

All info offices are closed on Christmas Day and New Year's Day. For more information: tel. +32 (0)50 44 46 46, toerisme@brugge.be, www.brugge.be

🗄️ Lockers

Station (railway station)
Stationsplein

25 Historium
Markt 1

Market days

» **Mondays**
8.00 a.m.-1.30 p.m. | Onder de Toren - Lissewege | miscellaneous
» **Wednesdays**
8.00 a.m.-1.30 p.m. | Markt | food and flowers
» **Fridays**
8.00 a.m.-1.30 a.m. | Market Square - Zeebrugge | miscellaneous

» **Saturdays**
8.00 a.m.-1.30 p.m. | 't Zand and Beursplein | miscellaneous
» **Sundays**
7.00 a.m.-2.00 p.m. | Veemarkt, Sint-Michiels | miscellaneous
» **Tuesdays to Saturdays**
8.00 a.m.-1.30 p.m. | Vismarkt | fish
» **Daily**
8.00 a.m.-7.00 p.m. | Vismarkt | artisanal products
» **Saturdays, Sundays, public holidays and bridge days in the period 15/3 to 15/11 + also on Fridays in the period June-September**
10.00 a.m.-6.00 p.m. | Dijver | antique, bric-a-brac and crafts

Money

Most of the banks in Bruges are open from 9.00 a.m. to 12.30 p.m. and from 2.00 p.m. to 4.30 p.m. Many branch offices are also open on Saturday morning, but on Sunday they are all closed. There are cash points in several shopping streets, on the Markt (Market Square),'t Zand, Simon Stevinplein, Stationsplein (Railway station Square) and on the Bargeplein (Barge Market). You can withdraw cash from these machines at any time of the day or night, using your Visa, Eurocard or Mastercard. Currency can be exchanged in every bank or in an exchange office.
» **Goffin Change**
Steenstraat 2 | City map: E8
» **Pillen R.W.J.**
Rozenhoedkaai 2 | City map: F8
Vlamingstraat 11B | City map: E7
» **New Best Money Change**
Sint-Amandsstraat 5 | City map: E8

Opening hours

Most shops open their doors at 10.00 a.m. and close at 6.00 p.m. or 6.30 p.m from Monday to Saturday. Some shops are also open on Sunday afternoon. Cafés and restaurants have no (fixed) closing hour. Sometimes they will remain open until the early hours of the morning and sometimes they will close earlier: it all depends on the number of customers.

Parking

Bruges is a compact city. Most places of interest are within walking distance of your accommodation. In order to keep the historic city centre attractive and accessible, aboveground parking in the city centre is limited to a maximum of 4 hours in the Blue Zone and to 2 hours in the Pay&Display Zones. You can easily park your car in one of the underground car parks. The most inexpensive and largest car park is in front of the railway station (City map D13): you pay € 3.50 a day, bus transfer with De Lijn to and from the city centre for 4 passengers included. These buses leave every five minutes. The Park and Ride areas are situated within walking distance of the city centre. Here you can park your car for free and for a longer duration. The city centre is a stone's throw away on foot or by bus.

▶ Parking Centrum-Zand
CAPACITY > 1400
OPENING TIMES > Daily, 24 hours a day
PRICE > Maximum € 8.70/24hrs | hourly rate: € 1.20; from the second hour you pay per quarter

▶ Parking Centrum-Station
CAPACITY > 1500
OPENING TIMES > Daily, 24 hours a day
PRICE > Maximum € 3.50/24hrs | hourly rate: € 0.70

Post Offices

» **BPost Markt**
Markt 5 | City map: E8
» **BPost Beursplein**
Sint-Maartensbilk 14 | City map: B10

Public holidays

Belgium has quite a lot of public holidays. On these holidays most companies, shops, offices and public services are closed.
» 1 January (New Year's Day)
» 20 April (Easter Sunday) and 21 April (Easter Monday)
» 1 May (Labour Day)
» 29 May (Ascension Day)
» 8 June (Whit Sunday) and 9 June (Whit Monday)
» 11 July (Flemish regional holiday)
» 21 July (Belgian national holiday)
» 15 August (Assumption of Mary)
» 1 November (All Saints' Day)
» 11 November (Armistice Day)
» 25 December (Christmas)
» 26 December (Boxing Day)

Public transport
▶ 🚌 Bus
You can use public transport during your stay. De Lijn connects the railway station and the centre by a bus every five minutes. From Bargeplein (city map E13), close to the spot where the tourist buses stop, there are also frequent services to the station and the city centre. The most important city's bus stops are marked with a bus pictogram on the fold-out map at the back of this guide.

▶ Tickets
» **Advanced booking offices**
De Lijnwinkel, Stationsplein (railway station)
Info office 't Zand (Concertgebouw)
Various city centre bookshops, newsagents and department stores
» **Vending machines De Lijn**
De Lijnwinkel, Stationsplein (railway station)
Bushalte 't Zand
» **Information** www.delijn.be

Smoking
In Belgium there is a general ban on smoking in cafés, restaurants, the public areas in hotels (lobby, bar, corridors, etc.) and in all public buildings (train stations, airports, etc.). Those unable to kick the habit will usually find an ashtray just outside (often under shelter), so that they can puff away to their heart's content in the open air.

Swimming Pools
11 Interbad
INFO > Veltemweg 35, Sint-Kruis, tel. +32 (0)50 35 07 77, interbad@skynet.be; bus: no. 10 or no. 58, stop: Watertoren (water tower)

12 Jan Guilini
INFO > Keizer Karelstraat 41, tel. +32 (0)50 31 35 54, sportdienst@brugge.be; bus: no. 9, Stop: Visartpark

13 Olympia
INFO > Doornstraat 110, Sint-Andries; tel. +32 (0)50 39 02 00, olympiabad@west-vlaanderen.be, www.west-vlaanderen.be/olympiabad; bus: no. 25, Stop: Jan Breydel or no. 5, Stop: Lange Molen

All information about opening times is available at the ℹ information office Markt (Historium), 't Zand (Concertgebouw) or Stationsplein (Station, railway station).

Taxis
ℹ Whoever takes a taxi in Bruges with the logo 'info on the go' can enjoy all the benefits of a Certified Info Driver. As 'ambassadors' for Bruges, these taxi-drivers will tell you with great enthusiasm all about their native city and will help to put you in just the right mood for your city visit.
TAXI STANDS > Markt and Stationsplein
TARIFFS > The local taxi companies all use the same fixed rate tariffs (adjustments are possible throughout the year):
Bruges <> Brussels Airport: € 200.00
Bruges <> Brussels South – Charleroi Airport: € 250.00
Bruges <> Aéroport de Lille: € 140.00
Please note: when you want to take a taxi from one of the airports to Bruges, you can only benefit from the above tariffs if you book the taxi in advance.

Telephoning
If you want to phone someone in Bruges from abroad, you must first dial the country code (00)32, followed by the zone code 50, and then number of the person you want. To phone Bruges from inside Belgium, you dial 050 plus the number of the person.

Toilets
There are a number of public toilets in Bruges (see the fold-out plan at the back of the guide). Some are accessible for wheelchair users, others have baby-changing areas. You will also find free toilets in some of the larger department stores or at the station. When local people need the toilet, they often pop into a cafe or pub to order something small so that they can use the facilities there.

Travelling season
Although most visitors come to the city in the spring and summer months, Bruges has something to offer all year round. The misty months of autumn and winter are ideal for atmospheric strolls along the canals and the cobbled streets, before ending up in a cosy restaurant or cheerful pub. The 'cold' months are also perfect for undisturbed visits to the city's many museums and sites of interest, before again finishing up in one of those same restaurants or pubs! What's more, in January, February and March you can get great discounts on many accommodation outlets in Bruges.

Walking
in Bruges

» START	**i** 't Zand (Concertgebouw)
» DISTANCE	3 km
» FINISH	Saint John's Hospital

Walk 1

Bruges, proud World Heritage City

Bruges may be, quite rightly, very proud of her World Heritage status, but the city is happily embracing the future too! This walk takes you along world-famous panoramic views, sky-high monuments and centuries-old squares invigorated by contemporary constructions. One foot planted in the Middle Ages, the other one firmly planted in the present. This walk is an absolute must for first-time visitors who would like to explore the very heart of the city straight away. Keep your camera at the ready!

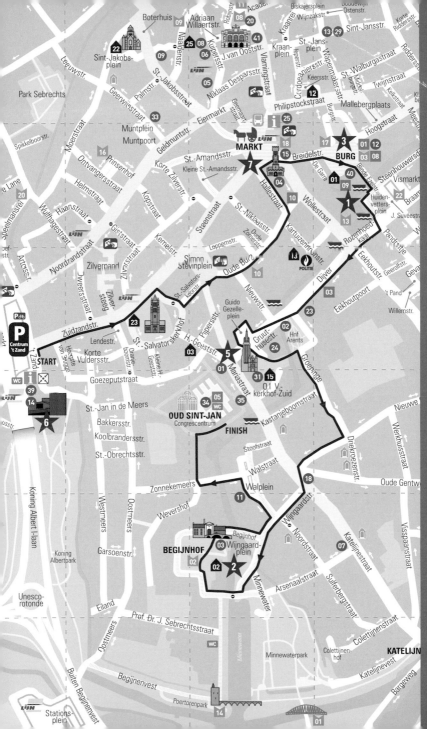

From 't Zand to Simon Stevinplein

This walk starts at the Tourist Information office **ℹ** 't Zand (Concertgebouw). 't Zand is dominated by the concert hall **14**, one of Bruges' most talked-about buildings. Clear-cut proof that this World Heritage city isn't afraid of the future. On the very top floor of this modern cube-shaped building you can find the Sound Factory, which is housed in the so-called Lantaarntoren (Lantern Tower) **39**. Don't forget to drop in at **ℹ** 't Zand (Concertgebouw) on the ground floor: here you will find all the necessary tourist information as well as expert advice on all cultural events.

Leave **ℹ** 't Zand (Concertgebouw) behind you, walk along the square and turn into Zuidzandstraat, the first street on the right. Saint Saviour's Cathedral **23** looms up ahead on your right after three hundred metres.

TIP

Why not call in at the Sound Factory and let those Bruges bells ring! And because the Sound Factory is located in the Lantern Tower at the very top of the Concert Hall, you can enjoy a superb panorama over the city while the bells play your very own carillon composition.

Bruges' oldest parish church is located on its original street level, i.e. lower than the present Zuidzandstraat. The street level gradually rose throughout the Middle Ages as people simply threw their refuse out onto the street where it was then flattened by passing carts and coaches. Inside Saint Saviour's, the church tower's wooden rafters can be lit. The cathedral treasury displays, amongst others, interesting copper memorial plaques, fine examples of gold and silver and paintings by Dieric Bouts, Hugo van der Goes and Pieter Pourbus.

Continue past the cathedral and walk down Sint-Salvatorskerkhof immediately on the right. Turn left into Sint-Salvatorskoorstraat. Simon Stevinplein opens up at the end of this street. This attractive square, lined with cosy restaurant terraces in summertime, is named after Simon Stevin, a well-known Flemish-Dutch scientist. His gracious statue naturally takes centre stage.

Markt and Burg

Continue down Oude Burg, a street in the right-hand corner of the square. Before long you will see the Cloth Halls **10** on your left. These belong to the Belfry **04**. You're allowed to cross the halls' imposing inner court between 8.00 a.m. and 6.00 p.m. during the week, and between 9.00 a.m. to 6.00 p.m. at weekends. The Markt is at the other end of the yard. If the gate is closed, turn back and walk down Hallestraat, which runs parallel to the Halls.

Walk II (see page 54) comments extensively on Markt.

Return to the Belfry **04** and walk down Breidelstraat, a traffic-free alley on the corner. Continue to Burg. Along the way on your right you will notice De Garre, a narrow alley. This may be the narrowest street in Bruges (try walking side by side here!), it nevertheless boasts a fair number of cosy cafés. Burg is the most majestic square in the city, so take your time to admire its grandeur. The main character in this medieval story is the City Hall **09** **40** (1376-1420), one of the oldest city halls in the Netherlands and a Gothic example for all its brothers and sisters that were built later, from Leuven to Oudenaarde and Brussels. Having admired its exterior, enter the impressive Gothic Hall and gaze in admiration at the polychrome floating ribs of the vaulted ceiling. Hiding on the right-hand side of this Gothic monument is the Basilica of

BURG: AN ARCHITECTURAL SYNOPSIS

Art lovers have already noticed that Burg projects a wonderful cross-section of stunning architectural styles. It is, indeed, a summing-up in one place of all the styles that have caught our imagination throughout the various centuries. From Romanesque (Saint Basil's Basilica) and Gothic (City Hall) by way of Renaissance (Civil Registry) and Baroque (Deanery) to Classicism (Mansion of the Liberty of Bruges). There's no need to go and dash all around Bruges to see it all!

01

the Holy Blood 01 , a mystical double chapel, below which sits the Romanesque Basilica of Saint Basil (1139 1149). One floor up is a basilica in Gothic revival style where the reliquary of the Holy Blood has been kept since time immemorial. Each year on Ascension Day, the reliquary is carried along in the Procession of the Holy Blood, a much-loved event that has been warming the hearts of the entire population from as early as 1304. Facing the basilica is the gleaming Renaissance façade of the erstwhile Civil Registry 03 (1534-1537, which now houses the City Archive 08 adjacent to the Liberty of Bruges 01 12 . Its showpiece is a splendid oak mantelpiece with an alabaster frieze (1529). Adjoining is the former mansion of the Liberty

of Bruges (1722-1727). It is from here that the country around Bruges was administered. After 1795 a court of justice was installed. It has been the city's administrative centre since 1988. Once upon a time Saint Donatian's Cathedral graced the spot directly in front of the City Hall. The church was torn down in 1799. Adjacent to it is the Deanery (1655-1666) 17 of the cathedral.

Fishy stories

Proceed to Blinde-Ezelstraat, the little street to the left of the City Hall. Don't forget to look back at the lovely arch between City Hall and Old Civil Registry 03 08 . Do you see Solomon? Left of him is the statue of Prosperity, to the right the statue of Peace.

According to legend, Blinde-Ezelstraat (Blind Donkey Street) owes its name to… a blind donkey. The house in the left hand corner hugging the water used to house a mill driven by a donkey. In order to preserve the poor animal from the

---

TIP

Take a breather on a bench on the Burg and enjoy the majestic splendour of this square in all its glory.

ing fish, fresh seafish was sold, a delicacy that only the rich could afford. Today you can still buy your fresh saltwater fish here every morning from Tuesday to Saturday.

Retrace your steps and turn left in front of the bridge towards Huidenvettersplein.

depressing thought that the only thing it had to do was turn endless rounds, a blindfold was put on the donkey. A new street name was born. Look left on the bridge: Meebrug is said to be the oldest bridge in Bruges.

The Vismarkt 22 opens up immediately past the bridge.
At first, fish was sold on one of the Markt's corners, but as the townspeople complained about the stench, the fishmongers were forced to move and sell their wares here. In the covered arcade (1821), specially erected for the purpose of sell-

Whereas the Vismarkt served the rich, Huidenvettersplein (Tanners Square) served the poor. No sea fish on the menu here, but affordable freshwater fish. The post in the middle of the square used to have a twin brother: in between the two posts hung the scales that the fish were weighed on. The large, striking building dominating the square used to be the guildhall of the tanners. Here they turned cow hides into leather. As this was a rather smelly job, it is no coincidence that the tanners' guildhall adjoined the fish market. Look out for the statuette adorning the corner of the hall. It's no surprise that the little fellow raises his nose.

Huidenvettersplein

Continue to Rozenhoedkaai.
Keep right.
Rozenhoedkaai is the most photographed spot in Bruges. So, take out your camera! This used to be the salt port. In the Middle Ages salt was as expensive as gold: it served to preserve food and to season dishes. A word like *salaris* (Dutch), *salaire* (French), salary still harks back to medieval times. The word derives from sal, which is Latin for salt. Roman soldiers' wages were paid in salt!

From Groeninge to the Bonifacius Bridge

Continue along Dijver.

Many centuries ago all manner of druids gathered on this holy spot to give praise to their gods and spirits. Along this atmospheric stretch of water, you will first find the College of Europe (numbers 9 to 11) **03**, an international postgraduate institution that focuses on European affairs, and then the Groeninge Museum (number 12) **23**, Bruges' most renowned museum. On display are world-famous masterpieces by Jan van Eyck, Hans Memling, Hugo van der Goes, Gerard David and many other Flemish Primitives. The museum also has a valuable collection of Flemish expressionists, neoclassical top notch paintings from the 18th and 19th centuries and post-war modern art. Overall, the museum shows a complete overview of Belgian and southern Dutch (Flemish) painting from the 15th to the 20th century. The museum entrance is reached through a few picturesque courtyard gardens. Would you like to find

---

🏠 ALMSHOUSES, THE QUICKEST WAY TO HEAVEN

These 14th-century dwellings were charitable institutions, sometimes set up by the guilds to lodge their elderly members, sometimes set up by widows or well-to-do burghers who wanted to ensure their place in heaven. For that purpose, each set of almshouses had its own chapel where the  occupants of the almshouses would be expected to send their prayers of thanks up to heaven. Practically all of the almshouses have been carefully restored and modernised and offer cosy living to today's elderly, whilst their small yet picturesque gardens and whitewashed façades offer welcoming peace and quiet to the present-day visitor. Feel free to enter these premises, but don't forget to respect their perfect tranquillity.
(On the map the Almshouses are indicated by 🏠)

out more about the Flemish Primitives? Then leaf through to the interview on page 108 with Till-Holger Borchert, the Groeninge Museum's chief curator.

Continue along Dijver. The entrance gate to the Gruuthuse Museum **24** is on your left just beyond the little bridge.
You learn more about Gruuthuse on page 52 (Walk II).

Continue to Guido Gezelleplein, then turn left in front of the Church of Our Lady **15** **31** and follow the narrow footpath to the picturesque Bonifacius Bridge.

TIP

If you visit the Gruuthuse Museum, make sure you check out the small, red velvet chapel – a kind of religious business seat – that looks out over the altar of the Church of Our Lady (Onze-Lieve-Vrouwekerk).

The crosses that you see all over the place don't belong to graves at all – they are crosses taken down from church steeples during the First World War to disorientate the enemy spies. The crosses have never been put up again. Close to the Bonifacius Bridge is Bruges' smallest Gothic window. Look up! It was through this window that the lords and ladies of Gruuthuse were able to peer down onto their private jetty. Across the bridge is the charming city garden 'Arentshof' of the Arentshuis **02**, an elegant 18th-century abode. The top floor houses work by the versatile British artist Frank Brangwyn. The ground floor is reserved for temporary exhibitions. Rik Poot's remarkable sculpture group in the garden represents the Horsemen of the Apocalypse: famine, death, revolution and the plague. A theme that appealed to the painter Hans Memling as well. Go through the garden gate to reach the Groeninge Museum **23**, where more work by Memling is displayed.

On to the Beguinage!

Leave the garden once more through the narrow garden gate and turn left into 'Groeninge,' a winding street. Turn right again at the intersection with Nieuwe Gentweg. Notice the Saint Joseph Almshouses (17th century) and the De Meulenaere Almshouses (1613). Continue down the street.

On the left-hand corner of Oude Gentweg and Katelijnestraat is the Diamond Museum **18**, Bruges' most glittering museum and the place to be for all lovers of bling. It goes without saying that an inspiring diamond museum simply couldn't be absent in the most romantic city of the western hemisphere!

Turn left into Katelijnestraat, then immediately right into Wijngaardstraat. Cross Wijngaardplein – a stopping place for coachmen. A little further on turn right onto the bridge beside the Sashuis (lockhouse) to enter the Beguinage. The bridge offers a fine view of the Minnewater.

The Minnewater used to be the landing stage of the barges or track boats that provided a regular connection between Bruges and Ghent. Today it is one of Bruges' most romantic beauty spots. Equally atmospheric, yet of a totally different nature, is the Beguinage. Although the 'Princely Beguinage Ten Wijngaarde' **02** , founded in 1245, is no longer occupied by beguines, but by nuns of the Order of Saint Benedict, you can still form

Wijngaardplein

an excellent picture of what daily life looked like in the 17th century at the Beguine's house **03** . The imposing courtyard garden, the whitewashed house fronts and blessed peace create an atmosphere all of its own. The entrance gate closes each day at 6.30 p.m. without fail. You have been warned!

Walk around the Beguinage and leave through the main gate. Turn left after

the bridge and left again to reach Walplein.

De Halve Maan , a brewery established as early as 1564, is at number 26 (at your left hand side). This is Bruges' last active city brewery. Their speciality is 'Brugse Zot' (Bruges' Fool), a spirited top-fermented beer made from malt, hop and special yeast. The name of the beer refers to the nickname of the Bruges townspeople, a name allegedly conferred upon them by Maximilian of Austria. In order to welcome the duke, the citizens paraded past him in a lavish procession of brightly-coloured merrymakers and fools. When a short time later they asked their ruler to finance a new 'zothuis' or madhouse, his answer was as short as it was forceful: 'The only people I have seen here are fools. Bruges is one big madhouse. Close the gates!'

A splendid finish at Saint John's Hospital

Turn left into Zonnekemeers. Once across the water, turn right to enter the area of Old St. John via the car park.
The former Hospital of Saint John (13th –14th century) 35 has a proud eight century-long history. The oldest documents even date back to the 12th century! Here, nuns and monks took good care of pilgrims, travellers and the sick. And people sometimes chose to die here. Hans Memling once was a patient here too. According to a much later legend, he

rewarded his benefactors with no fewer than six masterpieces
Right in front of the convent buildings of the old hospital complex you will come across The Veins of the Convent, a sculptural work by the contemporary Italian artist Giuseppe Penone. Or how history still feeds the present - what could be more appropriate for a World Heritage City like Bruges! Turn left at the corner and then go immediately right: in the open space of the courtyard you will find the herb garden and the entrance to the 17th century pharmacy, which is well worth a visit. The herb garden contains all the necessary ingredients for 'gruut' or 'gruit', including lady's mantle, myrtle and laurel. You can find an explanation of what *gruut* is in walk 2 on page 52.

Retrace your steps, turn left and walk through the passage.
The entrance to the imposing medieval hospital wards, its church, the Diksmuide attic and the old dormitory are just around the corner to the right.

» START	Guido Gezelleplein, Church of Our Lady
» DISTANCE	2,5 km
» FINISH	Prinsenhof

Walk 2

Bruges: B of Burgundian

When, during Bruges' Golden Age Philip the Bold, Duke of Burgundy, married Margaret of Dampierre, the daughter of the last Count of Flanders, the county of Flanders suddenly found itself belonging to Burgundy. As the Burgundian court liked to stay in Bruges, the port city became a magnet for noblemen, merchants and artists. They naturally all wanted to get their share of the city's wealth. Today the Burgundian influence is still strongly felt throughout Bruges. Let's discover a northern city with a southern character.

From Guido Gezelleplein to Markt

This square is named after the Flemish priest and poet Guido Gezelle (1830-1899). Take a seat on one of the square's benches and enjoy Gezelle's lovely statue and the side-view of the Church of Our Lady **15** **31**. Its one hundred and twenty-two metre high brick tower is sure proof of the craftsmanship of Bruges' artisans. Take a look inside and admire the rich art collection that includes Michelangelo's world-famous *Madonna and Child* and the 15th and 16th-century mausoleums of Mary of Burgundy and Charles the Bold. On your left is the striking residence of the lords of Gruuthuse, now the Gruuthusemuseum **24**. The tower and well were status symbols, and evidence of the Gruuthuse family's great wealth. They made their fortune from their exclusive rights on 'gruut', a herb mixture that, ages before hop, was used to

flavour beer. Louis of Gruuthuse not only commanded the army of Charles the Bold, he was also the personal bodyguard to Mary of Burgundy. A cultured man, he owned the Gruuthuse manuscript, a famous medieval codex containing amongst its many texts no fewer than 147 songs. The family's motto was *Plus est en vous* (There is more in you than you think). It's proudly displayed above the door of their residence.

Continue along the narrow footpath to the left of the church.

TIP

The impressive late-Gothic mansion on the corner of the Wollestraat, was built around 1500 on the instructions of Juan Perez de Malvenda, who at that time was the Consul of the Spanish Nation in Bruges. On the ground floor you can find a collection of all the things for which Belgium is famous: from a limitless choice of regional beers, through delicious biscuits and traditionally made jams, to fantastic old-fashioned sweets. The well-hidden terrace offers a magnificent view over the Rozenhoed Quay.

Look up immediately beyond the bend. Do you see the chapel that seems to hold the Gruuthuse Museum and the Church of Our Lady in a close embrace? As the lords of Gruuthuse were far too grand to mingle with the populace, they had their own private chapel high above the street, where they could follow Mass. This intimate place of worship can still be visited.

Retrace your steps, cross the attractive Gruuthuseplein and turn right into Dijver.
Number 12 is the Groeninge Museum 23 , Bruges' most famous museum. An interview with chief curator Till-Holger Borchert is on page 108. Further along Dijver is one of the locations of the College of Europe 03 , numbers 9-11, an international postgraduate institution that focuses on Europe.

Carry on down Dijver and turn left into Wollestraat.
Perez de Malvenda 13 is an impressive mansion on the corner of Wollestraat. This 15ᵗʰ-century town house, now a

food shop, has been restored from attic to cellar. Just before Markt are the Cloth Halls 10 , the Belfry's 04 warehouses and sales outlets. Facing the street, countless stalls were selling all sorts of herbs for medicinal purpose and potions. Indeed, Bruges being an important trading centre could be by then import a variety of herbs from all over Europe.

Markt, Bruges' beating heart
Wollestraat leads to Markt.
Markt is dominated by its Belfry 04 , for centuries the city's foremost edifice and the perfect look-out in case of war, fire or any other calamity. You can still climb to the top of the tower; but you will need to conquer no fewer than 366 steps to get there! Fortunately, there are a couple of places during your ascent where you can stop for a breather. Once at the top you will be rewarded with an unforgettable panoramic view. At the foot of the Belfry are the world's

THE CORRECT TIME

A gleaming terrestrial globe proudly sits on top of Boechoute, the house on the corner. This building from 1477 with its original lean-to-roof is now the Meridian 3 tearoom (on the Markt). When the Brussels to Bruges railway line was inaugurated, not all clocks in Belgium were set to the same time. The shortcoming was cured by the globe. At noon exactly, the sun coincided with its shadow through a hole in the globe. The line that was thus drawn can still be traced today thanks to a string of copper nails.

Markt

most famous chippies ('frietkoten')! The statue of Jan Breydel and Pieter de Coninck graces the middle of the square. These two popular heroes of Bruges resisted French oppression and consequently played an important part during the Battle of the Golden Spurs in 1302. Their statue neatly looks out onto the Gothic revival style Provincial Court (Markt 3) **18**.

Until the 18th century this was the place – now occupied by both the Post

---

TIP

As you are climbing your way to the top of the belfry tower, why not stop for a break at the vaulted treasure chamber, where the city's charters, seal and public funds were all kept during medieval times. You can make a second stop at the 'Stenen Vloer' (Stone Floor): here you will learn everything

The drum

you ever wanted to know about the clock, the drum and the carillon of 47 harmonious bells, which together weigh a staggering 27 tons of pure bronze. If you are really lucky, you might see the city's carilloneur in action, banging on the wooden keys that make the bells sound.

(Also read the interview with carilloneur Frank Deleu on page 100)

Office and the Historium **25** – where proudly stood the Water Halls (Waterhalle), a covered warehouse where goods were loaded and unloaded along the canals that ran alongside the square. Today the canals are still there, albeit underground.

Would you like a break? Then treat yourself to a coach ride and explore the city by horse and carriage for half an hour. Or maybe you prefer a fifty-minute city tour by minibus? You can continue your walk after your trip.

From Markt to Jan van Eyckplein

Ignore Markt on your left and continue straight ahead to Vlamingstraat. In the 15th century this used to be the harbour area's shopping street. A fair number of banks had a branch here, and wine taverns were two a penny. Each of these had a deep cellar where French and Renish wines could easily be stacked. In the medieval vaulted cellars of Taverne Curiosa (Vlamingstraat 22), the alcoholic atmosphere of those bygone days can still be inhaled. Halfway along Vlamingstraat is the elegant City Theatre **41** on your left. This royal theatre (1869) is one of Europe's best-preserved city theatres. Behind the Neorenaissance façade lie a magnificent auditorium and a palatial foyer. Papageno, the bird seller from Mozart's opera, *The Magic Flute*, guards the entrance. His score lies scattered on the square opposite.

Continue along Vlamingstraat and turn right into Kortewinkel just before the water.

04

TIP

Since as long ago as 1897, two green-painted mobile chippies have stood in front of the Belfry. It is definitely the best place in town to buy – and sell – chips, good for the annual consumption of several tons of fast food! The city's chip-sellers can bid once every two years for the right to stand on this lucrative spot. The highest bidder gets the contract. The stalls are open nearly every hour of the day and night, so that you never need to go hungry!

SWANS ON THE CANALS

After the death of Mary of Burgundy, Bruges went through some troubled times. The townspeople, enraged by new taxes Maximilian of Austria, Mary's successor, had imposed upon them, rose in revolt against their new ruler. As Maximilian was locked up in House Craenenburg on the market square, he helplessly witnessed the torture and eventual beheading of his bailiff and trusted councillor Pieter Lanchals (Long Neck). According to legend, once the duke had regained power, the citizens of Bruges were ordered to keep swans or long necks ('langhalzen') on the canals for all eternity.

Somewhat hidden from gazing eyes, Kortewinkel boasts a unique 16th-century wooden house front. It is one of only two left in the city (you will come across the other one further along this walk). Just a few metres on is another delicious discovery at number 10. The Jesuit

Monastery **09** has a magnificent secretive courtyard garden. Is its door open? Then walk in and enjoy its heavenly peace.

Kortewinkel turns into Spaanse Loskaai, the home port of the Spanish merchants in Burgundian times.

The picturesque bridge on your left is the Augustine Bridge, one of Bruges' oldest specimens, what with its seven hundred summers. The stone seats were originally intended to display the wares of the diligent sellers. The bridge affords an excellent view of the house in the right-hand corner, which connects Spanjaardstraat with Kortewinkel. This used to be not only a monastery but also a haunted house, so say the locals. When an amorous monk was rejected by a nun, the man murdered her and then committed suicide. Ever since they have been haunting that ramshackle building…

Continue along Spaanse Loskaai, go down the first street on your right and proceed to Oosterlingenplein.

During Bruges' Golden Age this was the fixed abode of the so-called 'Oosterlingen' or German merchants. Their imposing warehouse took up the entire left side of the square. Today the only remnant is the building to the right of Hotel Bryghia. Their warehouse must have been truly grand!

Beyond Oosterlingenplein is Woensdagmarkt. You will then find yourself on the square on which the statue of the painter Hans Memling attracts all attention. Turn right into Genthof. Here the second of two authentic medieval wooden house fronts draws attention. Notice that each floor juts out a little more than the next one. This building technique, which helped to avoid water damage, was consequently used in various architectural styles.

Burgundian Manhattan

Proceed to Jan van Eyckplein.
This was Burgundian Bruges' Manhattan, the place to be! Here ships docked, cargoes were loaded and unloaded and tolls were levied. In this unremitting hustle and bustle a cacophony of languages was heard above the din, the one sounding even louder than the other. What a soundtrack! Each business transaction required a few local sounds too, of course, as there always

had to be a Bruges broker present who would naturally pocket his cut. On the corner 16th-century Huis De Roode Steen (number 8) has been sparkling in all its glory since its restoration in 1877. At numbers 1-2 is the Old Tollhouse (1477) 06 21 , where all tollage was settled. To the left of this monumental building is Pijndershuisje, Bruges' narrowest dwelling. The house belonged to a pijnder or docker, a name that you can easily derive from its telling façade, that is if you keep your eyes peeled. The hunched 'pijnders' were employed to load and unload sacks and casks.

Continue along Academiestraat.
Right on the corner with Jan van Eyckplein is another remarkable construction, distinguished by its striking tower. This is Burghers' Lodge 15 , a kind of 15th-century private club where prominent inhabitants of Bruges could mix socially with foreign merchants. Hidden in a niche of this Burghers Lodge is the little Bruges' Bear, one of the city's most important symbols.

TIP

The Genthof has in recent years attracted a variety of different arts and crafts. There is a glass-blower, a poetry shop, a trendy vintage store and a number of contemporary art galleries. And on the corner you can find 't Terrastje, the café with probably the smallest terrace in Bruges.

 <!-- markers 06 15 21 -->

Proceed to Grauwwerkersstraat.
The little square connecting Acade-miestraat with Grauwwerkersstraat has been known as 'Beursplein' since time immemorial.

Here merchants were engaged in high-quality trade. The merchant houses of Genoa (later renamed 'Saaihalle' 08, and today Belgian Fries Museum 20), Florence (now De Florentijnen restaurant) and Venice (now Polare bookshop) once stood here side by side like brothers. In front of Huis ter Beurze (1276), the central inn 11, merchants from all over Europe used to gather to arrange business appointments and conduct exchange transactions. The Dutch word for stock exchange became 'beurs', derived from the name of the house. Many other

languages would take over this term, such as French (*bourse*) or Italian (*borsa*).

Turn into Grauwwerkersstraat and stop immediately in your tracks.
The side wall of Huis ter Beurze 11, and more precisely the part between the two sets of ground-floor windows, bears the signatures of the stonemasons. This way everybody knew which mason cut which stones and which mason remained to be paid. The house next-door to Huis ter Beurze, called the Little Beurze, still sits on its original street level.

Turn left into Naaldenstraat.
On your right, Bladelin Court 09 with its attractive tower looms up ahead. In the 15th century, treasurer of the Order of the

THE LITTLE BEAR OF BRUGES

When Baldwin Iron Arm, the first Count of Flanders, visited Bruges for the first time, the first creature he saw was a big 'white' bear. According to legend, all this happened in the 9th century. After a fierce fight the count succeeded in killing the animal. In homage to the courageous beast he proclaimed the bear to be the city's very own symbol. Today 'Bruges' oldest inhabitant' in the niche of the Burghers Lodge is festively rigged out during exceptional celebrations. The Bruges Bear is holding the coat of arms of the Noble Company of the White Bear, which was a kind of jousting club for local knights, founded shortly after Baldwin's famous victory over the original 'white' bear.

Golden Fleece Pieter Bladelin, portrayed above the gate whilst praying to the Virgin Mary, leased his house to the Florentine banking family of de Medici, who set up one of their branches here. Today the edifice belongs to the Sisters of Our Lady of Seven Sorrows. We highly recommend a visit. But make a reservation before you go, by phoning +32 (0)50 33 64 34 and admire the magnificent courtyard garden and the city's first Renaissance façade, embellished with two stone medallions representing Lorenzo de Medici and his wife Clarissa Orsini.

Somewhat further along, next to another ornamental tower, turn right into Boterhuis, a winding cobbled alley that catapults you back straight into the Middle Ages. Keep right, pass Saint James' Church and turn left into Moerstraat.

The Dukes of Burgundy and the vast majority of foreign merchants patronised Saint James' Church **22**. Their extrava-

PRINSENHOF GOSSIP

> As Philip the Good hadn't yet laid eyes on his future wife, he sent Jan van Eyck to Portugal to paint her portrait. This way the duke wanted to make certain he had made the right choice. The duke's ploy worked, because history teaches us that the couple had a happy marriage.

> Although the popular Mary of Burgundy incurred only a minor fracture due to her fall off her horse, the accident would eventually lead to her death at Prinsenhof. Back in those times there was no cure for inflammation.

> During the hotel renovation no fewer than 568 silver coins, minted between 1755 and 1787, were dug up. After some careful counting and calculations it is assumed that the energetic English nuns entrusted the coins to the soil so as to prevent the advancing French troops from stealing their hard-earned capital.

gant gifts have left their glittering mark on the interior.

Prinsenhof (the Princes' Court), home base of the Dukes of Burgundy

Turn left into Geerwijnstraat and carry on to Muntplein.
Muntplein (Coin Square) belongs to nearby Prinsenhof 16 . As you might have guessed, this was where Bruges' mint was situated. The statue *Flandria Nostra* (Our Flanders), which represents a noblewoman on horseback, was designed by the Belgian sculptor Jules Lagae.

At the end of Geerwijnstraat turn right into Geldmuntstraat. The walk's finishing point is Prinsenhof.

We end the walk on a highlight. Prinsenhof used to be the palace of the counts and dukes. This impressive mansion, originally seven times the size of what you see today, was erected in the 15th century by Philip the Good to celebrate his (third) marriage to Isabella of Portugal. When Charles the Bold remarried Margaret of York, a swimming pool and a zoological garden were added to the ducal residence. It is no surprise that Prinsenhof not only became the favourite pied-à-terre of the Dukes of Burgundy, but also the nerve centre of

TIP

Behind the street Boterhuis, at Sint-Jakobsstraat 26, you will find Cinema Lumière 09 , purveyor of the better kind of artistic film. In other words, the place to be for real film-lovers.

16

their political, economic and cultural ambitions. Both Philip the Good (d.1467) and Mary of Burgundy (d.1482) breathed their last here. After the death of the popular Mary of Burgundy the palace's fortunes declined, until it eventually ended up in private hands. In the 17th century, English nuns converted it into a boarding school for girls of well-to-do parents. After the nuns had gone, the complex changed ownership many times. Nowadays you can stay in the Prinsenhof Castle in true princely style.

TIP

Whoever wants to get a really good impression of the magnificence of this city castle and its elegant gardens should follow the signs in the Ontvangersstraat to the hotel car park at the Moerstraat 46. Of course, you can always treat yourself – and your nearest and dearest – to a princely drink in the bar of the Dukes' Palace Hotel: the perfect way to enjoy the grandeur and luxury of the complex.

» START	Choco-Story (Wijnzakstraat 2)
» DISTANCE	4 km
» FINISH	Café Vlissinghe (Blekersstraat)

Walk 3

Strolling through silent Bruges

Although the parishes of Saint Anne and Saint Giles are known as places of great tranquillity, the fact that they are off the beaten track does not mean that the visitor will be short of adventure. How about a row of nostalgic windmills? Or perhaps some unpretentious working-class neighbourhoods or a couple of exclusive gentlemen's clubs? Will you be able to absorb all these impressions serenely? Don't worry. After the tour we invite you to catch your breath in Bruges' oldest cafe!

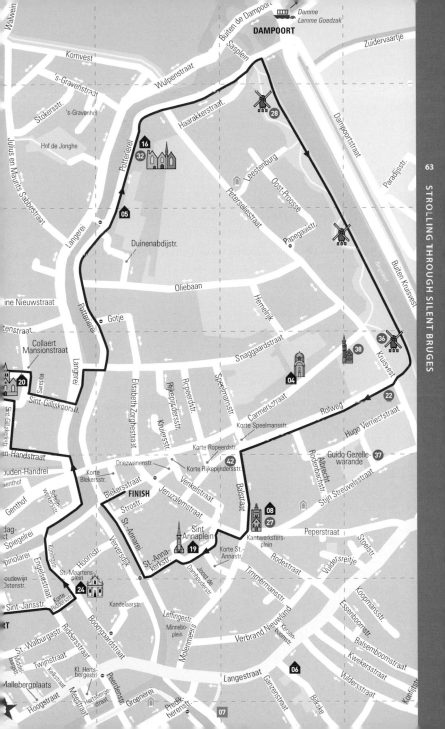

From Choco-Story to Gouden-Handstraat

Choco-Story (Museum of chocolate) **13** is the perfect starting point for the longest walk in this guide. This museum not only dips you in the yummy history of chocolate and cocoa, it also offers extensive chocolate tasting. If you wish, you can also buy your supplies here. No doubt the chocolate will help you to keep up a brisk pace! At the same address Lumina Domestica **29** contains the world's largest collection of lamps and lights. The museum also houses 6,000 antiques.

Turn left into Sint-Jansstraat, carry on to Korte Riddersstraat and turn left to Sint-Maartensplein.
Saint Walburgha's Church **24** rises up in all its magnificence right in front of you. This Baroque edifice (1619-1642) boasts a remarkable marble communion rail and high altar. At number 4 is the erstwhile Scottish warehouse.

Continue down Koningstraat to the bridge.
This bridge, which connects poetic Spinolarei with Spiegelrei, affords a lovely view of Oud Huis Amsterdam on your left. Today this historic town house (Spiegelrei 3) is an elegant hotel. This part of the city used to be mainly populated by the English and Scots. The English merchants even had their own steegere or stair where their goods were unloaded. The stair is still there, and the street

connecting it is appropriately called Engelsestraat. The dignified white school building (number 15) across the bridge was once a college of English Jesuits.

Saint Giles', home base of workmen and artists

Cross the bridge, turn right along

Spiegelrei and turn into Gouden-Hand-straat, the fourth street on your left.
In the 15th century Gouden-Handstraat and the parish of Saint Giles were known as the artists' quarter. Hans Memling may have lived a few streets further down in Sint-Jorisstraat; the fact of the matter is that Jan van Eyck had a studio in Gouden-Handstraat, and that his somewhat lesser known fellow artists also used to congregate in this neigh-bourhood.

Turn right into Sint-Gilliskerkstraat.
This street bumps into Saint Giles' Church  in the heart of the tranquil quarter of Saint Giles'. Initially a chapel, this house of God was upgraded to a parish church in 1258. In spite of its inte-rior in Gothic revival style and its superb paintings, the church takes on the ap-pearance of a simple, sturdy village church. Don't be misled. In and around the church countless famous painters were buried, such as Hans Memling (d.1494), in his time the best-paid paint-er, Lanceloot Blondeel (d.1561) and Pieter Pourbus (d.1564). Their graves and the cemetery may have disappeared, but their artists' souls still hover in the air.

Walk around the church and turn into Sint-Gilliskoorstraat.
Although the workmen's dwellings in these streets are rather small, they nevertheless display a bricked up win-dow. As it happened, a tax on windows was levied in 1800. As a consequence, a large number of windows were walled up.

BRUGES AND THE SEA

For centuries, Potterierei ensured the city's wealth. This canal ran to Damme where it was connected to a large lock, called 'Speie', which in turn was connected to the Zwin, a deep sea channel and tidal inlet. While Damme developed into an outport, Bruges grew into Northwestern Europe's greatest business centre of the Middle Ages. The arts flourished, culture thrived, prosperity seemed to be set for all eternity. The tide turned when Mary of Burgundy suddenly passed away. The relations between Bruges and the Burgundians turned sour and the Burgundian court left the city. The foreign merchants and their wealth followed in its wake. The Zwin silted up and Bruges lost her privileged commercial position. The city thus fell into a deep winter sleep.

From Potterierei to the vesten (ramparts)

Turn left into Langerei at the end of the street. Cross the lovely Snaggaardbrug, the first bridge you get to, into Potterierei. Turn left. (You will have to follow the canal for some time.)

After a fair distance along Potterierei is Bruges' Major Seminary (number 72) **05** on your right. A unique place with a lush orchard and meadows with cows at pasture. Between 1628 and 1642 a new Cistercian Abbey was erected here, which later on would achieve great fame for the wealth and erudition of its occupants. During the French Revolution, the abbey was brought under public ownership, and the abbot and monks were chased away. The 17th-century abbey buildings were first used as a military hospital and then as a military depot and a grammar school before they were eventually taken over by the Major Seminary in 1833. Up to the present day

the Seminary has been training catholic priests here. Just a few yards further down at number 79B is Our Lady of the Pottery) **16** **32**. Its history goes back to the 13th century. Diligent nuns used to treat pilgrims, travellers and the sick here. The Gothic church with its Baroque interior and its rich collection of works of art, accumulated by the hospital throughout the centuries, is a hidden gem that is certainly well worth a visit!

05

Carry on to the lock and turn right.
This idyllic spot is where the canal
Damse Vaart heads out across the other
side of the ring road towards the equally
romantic town of Damme. It's hard to
believe that this area around the canal
was once a scene of great controversy.
Up until the Eighty Years' War, Bruges
was connected to Sluis by way of
Damme. Ambitious Napoleon Bonapar-
te had the link with the tidal inlet of the
Zwin, the natural predecessor of the
Damse Vaart, dredged by Spanish pris-
oners of war so as to create a water-
course that would run all the way to Antwerp. His plan then was to develop the
port city of Antwerp into a naval base,
which would enable him to avoid the
English sea blockade. Napoleon's project left Damme cut in twain. The wild
plans of the little general were never
carried out in full, and by 1815 Napoleon's role in Flanders had come to an end.

TIP

Have we made you curious? Or do
you just like to do things the easy
way? If so, leave your bike and car at
home and 'all aboard' for a voyage on
the Lamme Goedzak 🚢 , the most
stylish way to reach the town of
Damme. Step back in time during
this nostalgic journey.
(For more information see pages 146-147)

However, the Dutch King William I also
saw the 'benefits' of a connecting canal,
and so excavation work was continued
until 1824. Belgian independence (1830)
meant that the project was finally termi-
nated, by which time it had reached as
far as Sluis.
Today the low-traffic bicycle path skirt-
ing the canal is a most attractive route
linking Bruges with Damme. The trip is
highly recommended, as it traverses

Sasplein

THE ARCHERS' GUILD:
120 MEN AND 2 QUEENS!

Although this used to be one of the poorer areas of the city for a very long time, the district includes two exclusive clubs. A greater contradiction cannot be found! Are you sitting comfortably out of harm's way on the slope of Sint-Janshuis Mill? Then look down on your left. There is Saint George's Guild **37**, a fellowship of crossbow men. Down on your right is Saint Sebastian's Guild **38** with its re-markably elegant tower. This guild goes back more than six centuries, which makes it unique in the world. The society numbers 120 male members exactly and two notable female honorary members: the Belgian queen Mathilde and the British queen. Ever since the exiled English king Charles II took up residence in Bruges in the 17th century, the city and the British Royal Family have always been closely associated. Whenever the British Royal Family is on a state visit to Belgium, so the rumour goes, they first of all pop in at the Saint Sebastian's Archers' Guild.

le plat pays, that flat country made famous by Jacques Brel in the moving song of that name. Imagine! In the middle of a unique polder landscape this truly poetic canal strip, bordered by lofty poplars bended down by eternal westerly winds.

Turn right and carry on along the Vesten (canals), which surround the city like a ring of green.
In the 16th century more than thirty windmills were turning their sails here. Today only four are left. In the 18th cen-tury the millers stood by helplessly when bread consumption took a dive and people started to consume more potatoes. Eventually steam machines would take over the millers' tasks. The Koelewei Mill **28** and Sint-Janshuis Mill **36** are open to visitors. The miller will happily explain the workings of his mill, and he will gladly give a milling demon-stration, too. Make sure you climb the slopes on which the Sint-Janshuis Mill and the Bonnechiere Mill (just next to the Kruispoort/Cross Gate **12**) proudly stand! The hills afford a fantastic pano-

ramic view of the city. This is the perfect spot to brush up on your amassed knowledge of Bruges. And there's more! Down below on your right is Verloren Hoek (the Lost Corner), now an authentic working-class district, but back in the 19th century an impoverished neighbourhood with such a bad reputation that even the police didn't dare enter its streets.

TIP

Interested in a little something 'extra'? Then go and take a look at the Albrecht Rodenbachstraat, another of the city's hidden gems. This green suburb *avant la lettre* offers an almost unbroken succession of step-gables and other fascinating facades, each fronted by a delightful little garden.

Silent Bruges

Descend down the slope and turn right into Rolweg.

Right on the corner is the Gezelle Museum **22**, the birthplace of Guido Gezelle (1830-1899), one of Flanders' most venerable poets. On display are handwritten letters, writing material and a deliciously peaceful garden with an age-old Corsican pine. Gezelle's parents worked here as gardener and caretaker, in exchange for which they and their family received free board and lodging. Little Guido grew up in these idyllic surroundings. He would eventually return to Bruges many years later and after many a peregrination. Upon his return he became curate of Saint Walburga's Church **24**. He also took over the running of the English Convent **04** (Carmersstraat 83-85), where he would die. These were his last words, reportedly: 'I have so loved hearing the birds singing.' Here, in this most verdant part of Bruges, we still know precisely what the priest and poet meant.

Turn into Balstraat, the second street on the left.

This picturesque working-man's alley houses the Folklore Museum (Volkskundemuseum) **42**. The 17th-century row of single-room dwellings, restored and converted into authentic artisans' interiors such as a milliner's, a confectioner's and a small classroom, will take you

---

TIP

If you feel like taking a break, you are welcome to rest your tired feet in the large, walled garden of the Folklore Museum. It is a delightful oasis of calm in the heart of the city, and even has its own outdoor bowling alley!

---

back to bygone days. The tower of the 15th-century Jerusalem Chapel **08** can easily be spotted from these premises. This chapel was commissioned by the Adornes, a prominent Bruges merchant family of Genovese origin. In 1470 Anselm Adornes collected one of his sons (the father had no fewer than sixteen children) in Padua to set off on a pilgrimage to the Holy Land. Upon his return to Bruges, Anselm decided to build an exact copy of the Church of the Holy Sepulchre. The result can be said to be remarkable, indeed! Immediately next to the chapel you can visit the Lace Centre **27** for a lace workshop or lace course. In 2014 the centre will be moving to the fully restored Lace School around the corner (Balstraat 16). Until then, it

this neighbourhood gradually became more upmarket, naturally the church did the same!

With the church behind you turn left into Sint-Annakerkstraat and then right into Sint-Annarei.
At the corner of the confluence of the two waterways one of Bruges' most handsome town houses is proudly showing off its Rococo credentials (Sint-Annarei no. 22). Sit yourself down on a shady bench and enjoy this exceptional prospect.

Retrace your steps for just a few yards and turn left into Blekersstraat next to the bridge.
Café Vlissinghe at number 2 is undoubtedly Bruges' oldest café. This has been a tavern since 1515. It is no surprise then that you will find oodles of ambiance here. It is therefore the perfect place to settle down and let the wonderful memories of your walk slowly sink in. A local beer will be your ideal companion. Cheers!

will occupy the row of renovated almshouses where up until fifty years ago lived lace-makers. If you enter the museum during a lacemaking demonstration (2.00-5.00 p.m.), then it will seem like you have gone back in time.

At the crossroads turn right into Jeruzalemstraat; then, at the church, left unto Sint-Annaplein.
The tiny square is dominated by the apparently simple Church of Saint Anne 19 . Her exterior may be austere, her interior on the other hand is one of Bruges' most splendid examples of Baroque architecture. If you are lucky, you might be able to catch a glimpse of this interior – notwithstanding the restoration work that is currently taking place. As

Know your way around Bruges

Bruges museums and places of interest

Some places are so special, so breathtaking or so unique that you simply have to see them. Bruges is filled to the brim with wonderful witnesses of a prosperous past. Although the Flemish Primitives are undoubtedly Bruges' showpiece attraction, museum devotees in search of much more will not be disappointed. Indeed, the Bruges range of attractions is truly magnificent. From modern plastic art by way of Michelangelo's world-famous *Madonna and Child* to a sumptuous Burgundian palace. It's all there for you to discover!

🎫 **01** Archeologiemuseum (Archaeological Museum)

This museum presents the unwritten history of Bruges. Its motto: feel your past beneath your feet. Discover the history of the city through different kinds of search and hands-on activities. A fascinating mix of archaeological finds, riddles, replicas and reconstructions shed light on daily life in times gone by, from the home to the workplace and from birth till death.

OPENING TIMES > Tuesday to Sunday, 9.30 a.m.-12.30 p.m. and 1.30 p.m.-5.00 p.m.; last admission: 12.00 a.m. and 4.30 p.m. (open on Easter Monday and Whit Monday)

ADDITIONAL CLOSING DATES > 1/1, 29/5 (afternoon) and 25/12

PRICE > € 4.00; 65+ and youngsters aged 12 to 25: € 3.00; children under 12: free; Brugge City Card: free

INFORMATION > Mariastraat 36A, www.museabrugge.be

🎫 **02** Arentshuis

In this elegant 18th-century town house with its picturesque garden the work of the versatile British artist Frank Brangwyn (1867-1956) is on display on the top floor. Brangwyn was both a graphic artist and a painter, as well as a designer of carpets, furniture and ceramics. The ground floor is the setting for temporary plastic art exhibitions.

OPENING TIMES > Tuesday to Sunday, 9.30 a.m.-5.00 p.m.; last admission: 4.30 p.m. (open on Easter Monday and Whit Monday)

ADDITIONAL CLOSING DATES > 1/1, 29/5 (afternoon) and 25/12

PRICE > € 4.00; 65+ and youngsters aged 12 to 25: € 3.00; children under 12: free; Brugge City Card: free; combination ticket with Groeninge Museum possible *(see page 82)*

INFORMATION > Dijver 16, www.museabrugge.be

🎫 ♿ **01** Basiliek van het Heilig Bloed (Basilica of the Holy Blood)

This double chapel consists of the Romanesque Basilica of Saint Basil (1139-1149) on the ground floor and the Basilica on the first floor, rebuilt in Gothic revival style in the 19th century. The Relic of the Holy Blood is kept in the Basilica.

The fully renovated treasury, with its numerous valuable works of art, is also well worth a visit.

OPENING TIMES > Daily, 9.30 a.m.-12.00 a.m. and 2.00 p.m.-5.00 5.00 p.m.; during the period 1/11 until 31/3 closed on Wednesday afternoon

PRICE > Double chapel: free; Treasure chamber: € 2.00; students: € 1.50; children under 13 and Brugge City Card: free

INFORMATION > Burg 13, tel. +32 (0)50 33 67 92, www.holyblood.com

02 02 03 Begijnhof (Beguinage)

The 'Princely Beguinage Ten Wijngaarde' with its whitewashed house fronts, tranquil convent garden and beguinage museum was founded in 1245. Today the nuns of the Order of Saint Benedict inhabit the site. The Beguinage entrance gate closes without fail at 6.30 p.m.

OPENING TIMES > Beguinage: daily, 6.30 a.m.-6.30 p.m.; Beguine's house: Monday to Saturday, 10.00 a.m.-5.00 p.m., Sunday 2.30 p.m.-5.00 p.m.

PRICE > Beguinage: free; Beguine's house: € 2.00; 65+: € 1.50; children aged 8 to 11 and students (on display of a valid student card): € 1.00; Brugge City Card: free

INFORMATION > Begijnhof 24-28-30, tel. +32 (0)50 33 00 11, www.monasteria.org

04 Belfort (Belfry)

The most important of Bruges' towers stands 83 metres tall. It houses a treasure chamber, an impressive clock mechanism and a carillon with 47 silvertoned bells. In 2012 the tower – the symbol of Bruges – was given a major face-lift. In the reception area, waiting visitors can now discover all kinds of interesting information about the history and working of this unique world-heritage protected belfry. Those who take on the challenge of climbing

the tower can pause for a breather on the way up in the old treasure chamber, where the city's charters, seal and public funds were kept during the Middle Ages, and also at the level of the clock or in the carilloneur's chamber. Finally, after a tiring 366 steps, your efforts will be rewarded with a breathtaking and unforgettable panoramic view of Bruges and her surroundings.

OPENING TIMES > Daily: 9.30 a.m.-5.00 p.m.; last admission: 4.15 p.m.

ADDITIONAL CLOSING DATES > 1/1, 29/5 (afternoon) and 25/12

PRICE > € 8.00; 65+ and youngsters aged 6 to 25: € 6.00; children under 6: free; Brugge City Card: free

INFORMATION > Markt 7, www.museabrugge.be

11 Brouwerij 'De Halve Maan' (Brewery)

The 'Halve Maan' (Half Moon) is an authentic and historic brewery in the centre of Bruges. This 'home' brewery is a family business with a tradition stretching back through six generations to 1856. This is where the Bruges city beer – the 'Brugse Zot' – is brewed: a strong-tasting, high-fermentation beer based on malt, hops and special yeast. There are guided tours of the brewery every day in a number of different languages. After the tour, visitors are treated to the blond version of the 'Brugse Zot'.

OPENING TIMES > During the period 1/4 until 31/10: daily, 11.00 a.m.-4.00 p.m. (Saturday till 5.00 p.m.), guided tours every hour; during the period 1/11 until 31/3:

Monday to Friday, guided tour at 11.00 a.m. & 3.00 p.m.; Saturday 11.00 a.m.-5.00 p.m. and Sunday 11.00 a.m.-4.00 p.m., guided tours every hour. Consult the website during holiday periods for the correct hours of opening.

ADDITIONAL CLOSING DATES > 1/1, 6/1 to 10/1, 13/1 to 17/1, 20/1 to 24/1, 24/12 and 25/12

PRICE > Including refreshment: € 7.50; children aged 6 to 12: € 3.75; Brugge City Card: free

INFORMATION > Walplein 26, tel. +32 (0)50 44 42 22, www.halvemaan.be

🚻 ♿ 01 03 08 12 Brugse Vrije (Liberty of Bruges)

From this mansion, erected between 1722 and 1727, Bruges' rural surroundings were governed. The building functioned as a court of justice between 1795 and 1984. Today the city archives are stored here. They safeguard Bruges' written memory. The premises also boast an old assize court and a renaissance hall with a monumental 16th-century timber, marble and alabaster mantelpiece made by Lanceloot Blondeel.

OPENING TIMES > Daily: 9.30 a.m.-12.30 p.m. and 1.30 p.m.-5.00 p.m.; last admission: 12.00 a.m and 4.30 p.m.

ADDITIONAL CLOSING DATES > 1/1, 29/5 (afternoon) and 25/12

PRICE > Including City Hall visit: € 4.00; 65+ and youngsters aged 12 to 25: € 3.00; children under 12: free; Brugge City Card: free

INFORMATION > Burg 11A, www.museabrugge.be

🚻 13 Choco-Story (Chocolate Museum)

The museum dips its visitors in the history of cocoa and chocolate. From the Maya and the Spanish conquistadores to the chocolate connoisseurs of today. A chocolate hunt gives children the chance to discover the museum. Chocolates are made by hand and sampled on the premises.

OPENING TIMES > Daily: 10.00 a.m.-5.00 p.m.; last admission: 4.15 p.m.

ADDITIONAL CLOSING DATES > 1/1, 6/1 to 17/1, 24/12, 25/12 and 31/12

PRICE > € 7.00; 65+ and students: € 6.00; children aged 6 to 11: € 4.00; children un-

der 5: free; Brugge City Card: free; several combination tickets possible

(see page 91)

INFORMATION > Wijnzakstraat 2, tel. +32 (0)50 61 22 37, www.choco-story.be

🏛 ⑮ Museum-Gallery Xpo Salvador Dalí

Admire the fantastic collection of worldfamous graphic works and sculptures of the famous artist Dalí. All the works are originals, whose authenticity has been confirmed by Gala-Salvador Dalí Foundation in Spain. An audio-guide (Dutch, French or English) leads you through the collection, which is presented in a sensational Daliesque décor of mirrors and shocking pink.

OPENING TIMES > Daily: 10.00 a.m.-6.00 p.m.

ADDITIONAL CLOSING DATES > 1/1 and 25/12

PRICE > € 10.00; 65+ and students: € 8.00; children under 12: free; audio-guide (available in 3 languages): € 2.00; Brugge City Card: free; several combination ticket possible *(see page 91)*

INFORMATION > Markt 7, tel. +32 (0)50 33 88 44, www.dali-interart.be

🏛 ⑱ Diamantmuseum Brugge (Bruges Diamond Museum)

Did you know that the technique of cutting diamonds was first applied in Bruges more than 500 years ago? The Bruges Diamond Museum tells this story in a series of fascinating exhibition displays. And there is a live demonstration of diamond cutting each day – a memorable experience, not to be missed! In the diamond laboratory, microscopes and other equipment allow visitors, both young and old alike, to discover the true beauty of diamonds – now one of Belgium's leading export products! – in all their many forms.

OPENING TIMES > Daily, 10.30 a.m. - 5.30 p.m. All year round there is a diamond-cutting demonstration at 12.15 p.m. each day; during the weekends, Belgian school holidays and the period 1/4 to 31/10 there is an extra demonstration at 3.15 p.m. (visitors need to be present 15 minutes in advance).

ADDITIONAL CLOSING DATES > 1/1, 6/1 to 17/1, 24/12 and 25/12

PRICE > Museum: € 7.00, museum + diamond-cutting demo: € 9.50; 65+ > museum: € 6.00, museum +

diamond-cutting demo: € 9.00; children 6 to 12 years and holders of a student card > museum: € 5.00, museum + diamond-cutting demo: € 8.00; children under 6: free; Brugge City Card: free; a combi-ticket is possible *(see page 91)*
INFORMATION > Katelijnestraat 43, tel. +32 (0)50 34 20 56, www.diamondmuseum.be

08 20 Frietmuseum (Belgian Fries Museum)

This didactical museum sketches the history of the potato, Belgian fries and the various sauces and dressings that accompany this most delicious and most famous of Belgian comestibles. The museum is housed in Saaihalle, one of Bruges' most attractive buildings.
OPENING TIMES > Daily: 10.00 a.m.-5.00 p.m.; last admission: 4.15 p.m.
ADDITIONAL CLOSING DATES > 1/1, 6/1 until 17/1, 24/12, 25/12 and 31/12
PRICE > € 6.00; 65+ and students: € 5.00;

children aged 6 to 11: € 4.00; children under 6: free; Brugge City Card: Free; combination ticket possible *(see page 91)*
INFORMATION > Vlamingstraat 33, tel. +32 (0)50 34 01 50, www.frietmuseum.be

07 21 Gentpoort (Gate of Ghent)

The Gate of Ghent is one of four remaining medieval city gates. An entrance for foreigners, a border with the outside world for the townspeople of Bruges. The gate was a part of the city's defences as well as a passageway for the movement of produce and merchandise.
OPENING TIMES > Thursday to Sunday, 9.30 a.m.-12.30 p.m. and 1.30 p.m.-5.00 p.m.; last admission: 12.00 a.m. and 4.30 p.m.
ADDITIONAL CLOSING DATES > 1/1, 29/5 (afternoon) and 25/12
PRICE > € 4.00; 65+ and youngsters aged 12 to 25: € 3.00; children under 12: free; Brugge City Card: free

INFORMATION > Gentpoortvest,
www.museabrugge.be

🏛♿ **22** Gezellemuseum (Gezelle Museum)

This museum, dedicated to the life and work of Guido Gezelle (1830-1899), is incorporated in the house where the famous Flemish poet was born. The museum doesn't only focus on the life and oeuvre of the great Flemish poet, it also houses temporary exhibitions on creative writing. Adjacent to the house is a romantic garden, where Jan Fabre's *The Man Who Gives Fire* is bound to catch your eye.

OPENING TIMES > Tuesday to Sunday:
9.30 a.m.-12.30 p.m. and 1.30 p.m.-
5.00 p.m.; last admission: 12.00 a.m. and
4.30 p.m. (open on Easter Monday and
Whit Monday)

ADDITIONAL CLOSING DATES >
1/1, 29/5 (afternoon) and 25/12
PRICE > € 4.00; 65+ and youngsters aged
12 to 25: € 3.00; children under 12: free;
Brugge City Card: free
INFORMATION > Rolweg 64,
www.museabrugge.be

🏛♿ **23** Groeningemuseum (Groeninge Museum)

The Groeninge Museum offers a varied overview of the history of Belgian plastic arts. Although the Flemish Primitives are a high point, you will also marvel at top 18th and 19th-century neoclassical pieces, masterpieces from Flemish Expressionism and post-war modern art.

OPENING TIMES > Tuesday to Sunday:
9.30 a.m.-5.00 p.m.; last admission:
4.30 p.m. (open on Easter Monday
and Whit Monday)

ADDITIONAL CLOSING DATES >
1/1, 29/5 (afternoon) and 25/12
PRICE > Including Arentshuis: € 8.00;
65+ and youngsters aged 12 to 25: € 6.00;
children under 12: free; Brugge City
Card: free
INFORMATION > Dijver 12,
www.museabrugge.be

24 Gruuthusemuseum (Gruuthuse Museum)

A royal welcome awaits you at this opulent city palace of the lords of Gruuthuse. The museum contains all manner
of objects that shed light on everyday
life between the 15th and 19th centuries.
One of the major attractions is the Hall
of Honour with its tapestries, impressive
fireplace and richly decorated rafters, all
witnessing the wealth and affluence of
the lords of Gruuthuse.
OPENING TIMES > Tuesday to Sunday:
9.30 a.m.-5 p.m.; last admission: 4.30 p.m.
(open on Easter Monday and Whit Mon-

day). During the second half of 2014 the
museum will be closed to the public for
restoration works.
ADDITIONAL CLOSING DATES >
1/1, 29/5 (afternoon) and 25/12
PRICE > € 8.00; 65+ and youngsters aged
12 to 25: € 6.00; children under 12: free;
Brugge City Card: free

INFORMATION > Dijver 17,
www.museabrugge.be

Historium Bruges

What was it like to live in Bruges during the Golden Century? The Historium allows you to find out for yourself! In seven themed rooms, where beautiful decoration, film, music and special effects are effortlessly blended together, all your senses will be engaged and you will follow (via an audio-guide in your own language) an exciting love story that leads you through the streets of the great medieval city. Take a walk around the port of 15th century-Bruges, take a look in the studio of the great painter Jan van Eyck and inhale the atmosphere of the city's streets. Let yourself be shocked and amused by the exotic fragrances and bawdy laughter in the bath house or take a spectacular flight over medieval Bruges. Afterwards, can make your way to the 'Duvelorium' (Grand Beer Cafe on the first floor) or to the panoramic terrace, where you can relive your experiences

and enjoy an unparalleled view over the Market Square.

OPENING TIMES > Daily, 10.00 a.m.-6.00 p.m (last admission: 5.00 p.m.)
ADDITIONAL CLOSING DATES >
1/1 and 25/12
PRICE > Including audio-guide (available in 9 languages): € 11.00; students (on display of a valid student card): € 9.00; children aged 2 tot 14: € 5.50; Brugge City Card: free; Family Pass (2 adults and max. 3 children aged 2 to 14): € 30.00; several combination tickets possible *(see page 91)*
INFORMATION > Markt 1, tel. +32 (0)50 27 03 11, www.historium.be

09 Hof Bladelin (Bladelin Court)

In around 1440 Pieter Bladelin, treasurer of the Order of the Golden Fleece, commissioned the construction of Bladelin Court. In the 15th century the powerful Florentine banking family of De Medici set up a branch here. The stone medallion portraits of Lorenzo de Medici and his wife still grace the picturesque inner court, which was recently restored to its former glory.

OPENING TIMES > Inner court, rooms and chapel: Monday to Friday 10.00 a.m.-12.00 a.m. and 2.00 p.m.-5.00 p.m.; visits are only possible with a guide and by appointment, tel. +32 (0)50 33 64 34

ADDITIONAL CLOSING DATES >
All (Belgian) public holidays

PRICE > Inner court, rooms and chapel: € 5.00 (price guide not included)
Garden: € 2.00

INFORMATION > Naaldenstraat 19, tel. +32 (0)50 33 64 34

27 Kantcentrum (Lace Centre)

The Lace Centre is housed in a 15th century complex, which includes (amongst other things) the historic almshouses funded by the Adornes family, who also built the Jerusalem Chapel. In the lace workshops various demonstrations are given (2.00 p.m. -5.00 p.m.) and numerous training courses are held. In the adjacent shop, you can buy different types of lace and lace products. In 2014, the Lace Centre will move to new premises in the renovated lace school at Balstraat no. 16 (just around the corner), which was once used by the Apostoline Sisters. This new location will make it possible for the first time in many years to create a lace museum (on the ground floor) that is truly worthy of the name.

OPENING TIMES > Monday to Saturday: 10.00 a.m.-4.45 p.m.

ADDITIONAL CLOSING DATES >
All (Belgian) public holidays

PRICE > € 3.00; 65+, students (on display of a valid student card) and youngsters aged 7 to 18: € 2.00; children under 7: free; Brugge City Card: free

INFORMATION > Peperstraat 3A (later: Balstraat 16), tel. +32 (0)50 33 00 72, www.kantcentrum.eu

🎴 29 Lumina Domestica (Lamp Museum)

The museum contains the world's largest collection of lamps and lights. More than 6.000 antiques tell the complete story of interior lighting. From torch and paraffin lamp to light bulb and LED.

OPENING TIMES > Daily, 10.00 a.m.-5.00 p.m.; last admission: 4.15 p.m.

ADDITIONAL CLOSING DATES >
1/1, 6/1 to 17/1, 24/12, 25/12 and 31/12

PRICE > € 6.00; 65+ and students: € 5.00; children aged 6 to 11: € 4.00; children under 6: free; Brugge City Card: free; combination ticket possible *(see page 91)*

INFORMATION > Wijnzakstraat 2, tel. +32 (0)50 61 22 37, www.luminadomestica.be

🎴 ♿ 15 31 Onze-Lieve-Vrouwekerk (Church of Our Lady)

The 122 metres high brick tower of the Church of Our Lady is a perfect illustration of the craftsmanship of Bruges' artisans. The church displays a valuable art collection: Michelangelo's world-famous *Madonna and Child*, countless paintings, 13th-century painted sepulchres and the tombs of Mary of Burgundy and Charles the Bold.

OPENING TIMES > Monday to Saturday, 9.30 a.m.-5.00 p.m.; Sunday and Holy Days, 1.30 p.m.-5.00 p.m. Last admission: 4.30 p.m., tickets for the museum section are on sale in the south transept. The church and the museum are not open to the public during nuptial and funeral masses. Useful to know: restoration work is currently being carried out in the church.

ADDITIONAL CLOSING DATES >
Museum: 1/1, 29/5 (afternoon) and 25/12

PRICE > Church: free; museum: € 6.00; 65+ and youngsters aged 12 to 25: € 5.00;

children under 12: free; Brugge City Card: free

INFORMATION > Mariastraat, www.museabrugge.be

🔲 16 32 Onze-Lieve-Vrouw-ter-Potterie (Our Lady of the Pottery)

This hospital dates back to the 13th century, when nuns took on the care of pilgrims, travellers and the sick. Over the centuries, the hospital developed into a modern home for the elderly. The hospital wards with their valuable collection of works of art, monastic and religious relics and a range of objects used in nursing have been converted into a museum. The Gothic church with its baroque interior can also be visited.

OPENING TIMES > Tuesday to Sunday, 9.30 a.m.-12.30 p.m. and 1.30 p.m.-5.00 p.m.; last admission: 12.00 a.m. and 4.30 p.m. (open on Easter Monday and Whit Monday)

ADDITIONAL CLOSING DATES > 1/1, 29/5 (afternoon) and 25/12

PRICE > Church: free; museum: € 4.00; 65+ and youngsters aged 12 to 25: € 3.00;

children under 12: free; Brugge City Card: free

INFORMATION > Potterierei 79B, www.museabrugge.be

17 Onze-Lieve-Vrouw-van-Blindekenskapel (Chapel of our Lady of the Blind)

The Chapel of Our Lady of the Blind is supposed to have been erected in timber in 1305 through the agency of Robert of Bethune, Count of Flanders. The count had the chapel built after the Battle of Mons-en-Pévèle (1304) in gratitude for the Virgin Mary. The present chapel dates from 1651. The miraculous oaken image of Our Lady of the Blind is a *Madonna and Child* from 1415. Each year on 15 August the procession of Our Lady of the Blind winds its way through the streets of Bruges. In order to abide by the Solemn Oath, sworn during the battle of Mons-en-Pévèle, the citizens of Bruges have been devoting a so-called solemn oath-candle in the Church of Our Lady of the Pottery since 1305.

OPENING TIMES > Daily, 9.00 a.m.-5.00 p.m.

PRICE > Free

INFORMATION > Kreupelenstraat

🎥 ♿ 34 Expo Picasso

The historic area of the former Hospital of Saint John (Old Saint John's) hosts a permanent exhibition of more than 120 original works of art by Pablo Picasso. Admire the engravings and rare illustrations as well as the drawings and ceramics of the world-famous artist. The exhibition outlines the evolution in his work: from his Spanish period to cubism to surrealism. Also on display are some 200 works by artist friends of Picasso's, such as Rodin, Miró, Chagall, Renoir and Matisse and even a few paintings by Monet, Toulouse-Lautrec, Degas and Braque...

OPENING TIMES > Daily, 10.00 a.m.-5.00 p.m.

ADDITIONAL CLOSING DATES >

1/1, 6/1 to 31/1 and 25/12

PRICE > € 8.00; 60+ and youngsters aged 7 to 18: € 6.50; children under 7: free; Brugge City Card: free; combination ticket possible *(see page 91)*

INFORMATION > Old Saint John's, Mariastraat 38, tel. +32 (0)50 47 61 08, www.expo-brugge.be

🎥 ♿ 35 Sint-Janshospitaal (Saint John's Hospital)

Saint John's Hospital has an eight hundred-year-old history of caring for pilgrims, travellers and the sick. Visit the medieval wards where the nuns and monks performed their work of mercy and marvel at the impressive collection of archives, art works, medical instruments and six paintings by Hans Memling. Also worth a visit: the Diksmuide attic, the old dormitory, the adjoining custodian's room and the pharmacy.

OPENING TIMES > Museum: Tuesday to Sunday, 9.30 a.m.-5.00 p.m.; last admission: 4.30 p.m.

Pharmacy: Tuesday to Sunday, 9.30 a.m.-11.45 a.m. and 2.00 p.m.-5.00 p.m.; last admission: 4.30 p.m. (both open on Easter Monday and Whit Monday)

ADDITIONAL CLOSING DATES >

1/1, 29/5 (afternoon) and 25/12

PRICE > Including visit to the pharmacy: € 8.00; 65+ and youngsters aged 12 to 25: € 6.00; children under 12: free; Brugge City Card: free

INFORMATION > Mariastraat 38,
www.museabrugge.be

🏠 36 Sint-Janshuismolen (Mill)
🏠 28 Koeleweimolen (Mill)

Windmills have graced Bruges' ramparts
ever since the construction of the outer
city wall at the end of the 13th century.
Today four specimens are left on
Kruisvest. Sint-Janshuis Mill (1770)
is still in its original spot and still
grinding grain just like its neighbour
Koelewei Mill.

OPENING TIMES > Sint-Janshuis Mill: during the period 1/5 until 31/8: Tuesday to
Sunday, 9.30 a.m.-12.30 p.m. and 1.30
p.m.-5.00 p.m.; last admission: 12.00 a.m.
and 4.30 p.m. (open on Whit Monday)
Koelewei Mill: during the period 1/7
until 31/8: Tuesday to Sunday, 9.30 a.m.-
12.30 p.m. and 1.30 p.m.-5.00 p.m.; last
admission: 12.00 a.m and 4.30 p.m.

ADDITIONAL CLOSING DATE >
Sint-Janshuis Mill: 29/5 (afternoon)

PRICE > For both mills together: € 3.00;
65+ and youngsters aged 12 to 25:
€ 2.00; children under 12: free; Brugge
City Card: free

INFORMATION > Kruisvest,
www.museabrugge.be

♿ 23 Sint-Salvatorskathedraal (Saint Saviour's Cathedral)

Bruges' oldest parish church (12th-
15th century) has amongst its treasures
a rood loft with organ, medieval tombs,
Brussels tapestries and a rich collection
of Flemish paintings (14th-18th century).
The treasure-chamber displays a.o.
paintings by Dieric Bouts, Hugo van der
Goes and other Flemish Primitives. Useful to know: restoration work is currently
being carried out in the cathedral.

OPENING TIMES > Cathedral: Monday
to Friday, 10.00 a.m.-13.00 p.m. and
2.00 p.m.-5.30 p.m.; Saturday, 10.00 a.m.-
13.00 a.m. and 2.00 p.m.-3.30 p.m.; Sunday, 11.30 a.m.-12.00 a.m. and 2.00 p.m.-
5.00 p.m.; the cathedral is not open to
the public during masses
Treasury: daily (except Saturday),
2.00 p.m.-5.00 p.m.

ADDITIONAL CLOSING DATES >
1/1 (afternoon), 29/5 (afternoon),
24/12 and 25/12 (afternoon)

PRICE > Cathedral and Treasury: free

INFORMATION > Steenstraat, tel. +32 (0)50 33 61 88, www.sintsalvator.be

38 Schuttersgilde Sint-Sebastiaan (St. Sebastian's Archers Guild)

The Archers' Guild of Saint Sebastian goes back 600 years. A unique feat indeed! A visit includes the royal chamber, the chapel chamber and the garden.

OPENING TIMES > During the period 1/5 until 30/9: Tuesday, Wednesday and Thursday, 10.00 a.m.-12.00 a.m., Saturday, 2.00 p.m.-5.00 p.m.; during the period 1/10 until 30/4: Tuesday, Wednesday, Thursday and Saturday, 2.00 p.m.-5.00 p.m.

PRICE > € 3.00

INFORMATION > Carmersstraat 174, www.sebastiaansgilde.be

14 39 Sound Factory – Lantaarntoren

Why not pay a visit to the Sound Factory in the Lantaarntoren (Lantern Tower) at the Concertgebouw? Get to work with samples and sounds, and create your own compositions. The roof of the Lantaarntoren not only commands a unique view across the historic city centre, but gives you the opportunity to experiment with bells and sounds to your heart's content.

OPENING TIMES > Tuesday to Sunday, 9.30 a.m.-5.00 p.m.; last admission: 4.30 p.m. (open on Easter Monday and Whit Monday)

ADDITIONAL CLOSING DATES > 1/1, 29/5 (afternoon) and 25/12

PRICE > € 6.00; 65+ and youngsters aged 12 to 25: € 5.00; children under 13: free; Brugge City Card: free

INFORMATION > 't Zand 34, www.musea brugge.be en www.sound-factory.be

09 40 Stadhuis (City Hall)

Bruges' City Hall (1376) is one of the oldest in the Low Countries. It is from here that the city has been governed for more than 600 years. An absolute masterpiece is the Gothic Hall with its late 19th-century murals and polychrome vault. The adjoining historic hall calls up the city council's history with a number of authentic documents and works of art. A multimedia exhibition on the ground floor illustrates the evolution of the Burg square.

OPENING TIMES > Daily, 9.30 a.m.-5.00 p.m.; last admission: 4.30 p.m.

ADDITIONAL CLOSING DATES > 1/1, 29/5 and 25/12

PRICE > Including Liberty of Bruges: € 4.00; 65+ and youngsters aged 12 to 25: € 3.00; children under 12: free; Brugge City Card: free

INFORMATION > Burg 12, www.museabrugge.be

OPENING TIMES > Tuesday to Sunday: 9.30 a.m.-5.00 p.m.; last admission: 4.30 p.m. (open on Easter Monday and Whit Monday)

ADDITIONAL CLOSING DATES > 1/1, 29/5 (afternoon) and 25/12

PRICE > € 4.00; 65+ and youngsters aged 12 to, 25: € 3.00; children under 12: free; Brugge City Card: free

INFORMATION > Balstraat 43, www.museabrugge.be

42 Volkskundemuseum (Folklore Museum)

These restored 17th-century singleroom dwellings accommodate a.o. a classroom, a millinery, a pharmacy, a confectionery, a grocery and an authentic bedroom. Conclude your visit with a pleasant stroll in the garden and a thirst-quenching drink at 'De Zwarte Kat' (The Black Cat), the museum's tavern (closed between 11.45 a.m. and 2.00 p.m.). Lace collection in the exhibition attic.

WALLET-FRIENDLY MUSEUM SHOPPING!

» Brugge City Card

With the Brugge City Card you can visit 27 Bruges museums and other sites of interest completely free of charge. The Brugge City Card can be purchased from the info-offices [i] on 't Zand (Concert Hall), the Market Square (Historium), and the Station Square (Station). You can also buy this reduction card online via www.bruggecitycard.be. For more information, see page 12.

» Museum Pass

With the Museum Pass you can visit the different Musea Brugge locations as often as you like for just € 20.00 (www. museabrugge.be). Young people aged 12 to 25 pay just € 15.00. The pass is valid for three consecutive days and can be purchased at all Musea Brugge locations and at [i] 't Zand (Concertgebouw).

» Combination ticket Historium/Groeninge Museum

Experience the Golden Century of Bruges in the Historium, with the painting of *Madonna and Child with Canon Joris van der Paele* by Jan van Eyck as your leitmotif. Then see the masterpiece itself in the Groeninge Museum, along with the great works of many others of the so-called Flemish Primitives. This € 15.00 combi-ticket is only available in the Historium.

» Combination ticket Historium/City Tour

Discover the Bruges of the year 1435 in the Historium and afterwards explore the prettiest places in present-day Bruges with the City Tour: € 25.00 and children 6 to 11 years: € 14.00. This combi-ticket is only available in the Historium.

» Combination ticket Expo Picasso/Museum-Gallery Expo Salvador Dalí

Discover the works of two top artists for just € 15.00; 60+ and youngsters aged 7 to 18: € 11.00. This combi-ticket is only available in the museums in question.

» Combination ticket Choco-Story/Diamond Museum

Combine a tasty visit to Choco-Story with a dazzling look at the Diamond Museum. This combination ticket costs € 12.00. For sale at the abovementioned museums and at [i] 't Zand (Concertgebouw).

» Combination ticket Choco-Story/Lumina Domestica/Belgian Fries Museum

Visit these three museums at reduced rates.

- » Combination ticket (select 2 museums): adults: € 11.00; 65+ and students: € 9.00; children aged 6 to 11: € 6.00; children under 6: free
- » Combination ticket (3 museums): adults: € 16.00; 65+ and students: € 13.00; Children aged 6 to 11: € 9.00; children under 6: free

These combination tickets are for sale at the above-mentioned museums and at [i] 't Zand (Concertgebouw).

Culture and amusement

The city's high-quality cultural life flourishes as never before. Devotees of modern architecture stand in awe of the Concertgebouw (Concert hall) whilst enjoying to the full an international top concert or an exhilarating dance performance. Romantic souls throng the elegant City Theatre for an unforgettable night. Jazz enthusiasts feel at home at Art Centre De Werf, whereas MaZ is the place to be for young people.

🏛️ ♿ **14** Concertgebouw (Concert Hall)

The impressive Concert Hall with its 1,289 seats and the intimate Chamber Music Hall with its 322 seats serve a delightful mix of music, musical theatre and contemporary dance of international quality. The acoustics and intimate comfort of both halls are exceptional.
Brugge City Card: 30% discount on productions marked in the free monthly events@brugge magazine.
INFORMATION > 't Zand 34, tel. +32 (0)70 22 33 02 (ticket line: Monday-Friday, 4.00 p.m.-6.30 p.m.), www.concertgebouw.be

🏛️ ♿ **41** Stadsschouwburg (City Theatre)

The Bruges City Theatre (1869) is one of the best-preserved theatres of its kind in Europe and was fully restored in 2001. The sober neo-Renaissance facade of this royal theatre conceals a palatial foyer and an equally magnificent auditorium. This outstanding infrastructure is regularly used by the Bruges Cultural Centre for performances of contemporary dance and theatre (both national and international productions) and for concerts of various kinds.
Brugge City Card: 30% discount on productions marked in the free monthly events@brugge magazine.
INFORMATION > Vlamingstraat 29, tel. +32 (0)50 44 30 60 (Monday to Friday, 1.00 p.m.-6.00 p.m. Saturday 10.00 a.m.-1.00 p.m.), www.ccbrugge.be

🏛️ ♿ **30** Magdalenazaal (MaZ, Magdalena Concert Hall)

Its 'black-box' architecture means that the MaZ is the ideal location for youth events. The Bruges Cultural Centre and the Cactus Music Festival both organize pop and rock concerts here. Major artists from the world of music and more intimate club talents can all 'do their own thing' in the MaZ. Rising stars in the theatrical and dance arts also perform in this perfect setting. Children's and family events are regular features on the programme.
Brugge City Card: 30% discount on productions marked in the free monthly events@brugge magazine.
INFORMATION > Magdalenastraat 27, Sint-Andries, tel. +32 (0)50 44 30 60 (Monday to Friday, 1.00 p.m.-6.00 p.m., Saturday, 10.00 a.m.-1.00 p.m.), www.ccbrugge.be

🏛️ ♿ **17** De Werf (Art Centre)

De Werf Cultural Centre has an excellent reputation in the jazz milieu and is a favourite venue for many Belgian and foreign jazz musicians. From the beginning of October to the end of May, there is a free jam session in the foyer on every second Monday of the month. De Werf is also a great place to pick up a theatre production or some other exciting podium performance. In short, this is a setting where people create, produce, present and are inspired!
Brugge City Card: 25% discount on productions marked in the free monthly events@brugge magazine.
INFORMATION > Werfstraat 108, tel. +32 (0)50 33 05 29, www.dewerf.be

What's on the programme?

The following list is a summary of the most important annual events in Bruges. At the info offices [i] on the Markt (Historium), 't Zand (Concertgebouw) and the Stationsplein (station) you can pick up a free copy of **events@brugge** the monthly magazine of events in Bruges. And, of course, for a detailed events calendar you can always consult the website at www.brugge.be.

January

Bach Academie

The fourth Bruges Bach Academy focuses on the young Bach and his time in Weimar and Köthen. The Freiburger Baroque Orchestra will perform the *Brandenburg Concertos* and there is a special place on the podium reserved for young violin talent. The festival starts and ends with a concert by Collegium Vocale Ghent.
INFORMATION > www.concertgebouw.be

February

Brugs Bierfestival
(Bruges Beer Festival)

For a full weekend the Beurshalle (Exhibition Hall) is the place to be if you want to learn more about Belgian beers, both old and new.
INFORMATION >
www.brugsbierfestival.be *(Read more in the interview with Bob Eck on page 132)*

Reismarkt (Travel Market)

An alternative travel fair in the City Halls. Under the motto 'Travellers help travellers', enthusiastic globetrotters exchange a wide range of tips and information about almost every type of travel and every destination you can think of.
INFORMATION > www.wegwijzer.be

March

Brugge Culinair (Culinary Bruges)

An exhibition for gourmets and gastronomes in the Oud-Sint-Jan complex. Free entrance.
INFORMATION > www.bruggeculinair.be

Ronde van Vlaanderen
(Tour of Flanders)

This historic and world-famous race for professional cyclists will be contested for the 98th time in 2014. The start is on the Markt.
INFORMATION >
www.rondevanvlaanderen.be

April

Mooov filmfestival

This 10-day film festival, screened in Cinema Lumière, shows the best new films from Africa, Asia and South America.
INFORMATION > www.mooov.be

Erfgoeddag (Heritage Day)

Throughout Flanders hidden heritage gems open their doors to the general public. Each year there is a different theme.
INFORMATION > www.erfgoeddag.be

May

Meifoor (May Fair)

For three fun-filled weeks some 90 fairground attractions 'take over' 't Zand, the Beursplein, the Koning Albert Park and the Simon Stevinplein.

Ascension Day – Heilig Bloedprocessie (Procession of the Holy Blood)

First held in 1304, this popular procession through the streets of the city depicts scenes from the Old and New Testaments.

(Read more in the box text)

Dwars door Brugge (The Great Bruges Run)

Tens of thousands of runners set off on a 15-kilometre run through Bruges.
INFORMATION > www.brugge.be

Airbag festival

The previous five editions have shown that the international Airbag accordion festival more than deserves its place in the Bruges events calendar. The festival offers a balanced combination of festive performances and easy-listening concerts.
INFORMATION >
www.ccbrugge.be/airbag

June

Feest in 't Park (Party in the Park)

A free, family-friendly festival in the Minnewater Park, with a children's world village, workshops, world cooking and plenty of music, theatre and dance.
INFORMATION > www.feestintpark.be

A CENTURIES-OLD PROCESSION

Every year on Ascension Day, under the watchful eye of a huge public, the Holy Blood Procession passes through the streets of Bruges city centre. In the first two parts of the procession, members of the religious community, various brotherhoods and numerous costumed groups play out well-known scenes from the Bible: from Adam and Eve in the Garden of Eden to the Passion of Christ. Next comes the story of Thierry of Alsace, Count of Flanders, who was awarded a few drops of the blood of Jesus by the patriarch of Jerusalem during the Second Crusade in 1146. This priceless relic was brought back to Bruges in a crystal bottle in 1150, since when believers have been able to revere the Holy Blood in the basilica of the same name. The final part of the procession is dedicated to the public veneration of the Holy Blood. Preceded by the Noble Fraternity of the Holy Blood, two prelates carry the reliquary through the city.

July

Zandfeesten (Zand Festival)
Flanders' largest antiques and second-hand market on 't Zand and in the adjacent King Albert Park attracts bargain-hunters from far and wide.

Cactusfestival
An atmospheric open-air music festival, which offers a cocktail of rock, reggae, world music and dance.
INFORMATION > www.cactusfestival.be

Navy Days
In Zeebrugge, under the watchful eye of sailors from home and abroad, you can hop from one impressive ship to another during this two-day regatta. With numerous free exhibitions and demonstrations.
INFORMATION > www.mil.be/navycomp

Brugge Tripel Dagen (Bruges Triple Days)
Three days of free musical fun and entertainment, with well-known Flemish stars and 'Vlaanderen Zingt' (Flanders Sings), a sing-along happening for the general public.
INFORMATION >
www.bruggetripeldagen.be

'Klinkers'
Two weeks of free concerts, outdoor cinema, comedy, dancing ('Benenwerk') and children's programme ('Klinkers for Kids') at unforgettable locations in Bruges' city centre.
INFORMATION > www.klinkers-brugge.be

August

Zandfeesten (Zand Festival)
Antiques and second-hand market on 't Zand (see above).

MAfestival
Each year this highly respected festival of ancient music – MA stands for Musica Antiqua – continues to attract the world's top performers to Bruges and Bruges' wet- and woodlands.
INFORMATION > www.mafestival.be

Lichtfeest (Festival of Light)
Lissewege, the white village, lights up the night with pyrotechnic displays, atmospheric music and thousands of candles.
INFORMATION > www.bruggeplus.be

September

Open Monumentendag (Open Monument Day)
In 2014 many of Flanders' greatest historical monuments will open their doors to the general public for the 26th successive year.
INFORMATION >
www.openmonumenten.be

'Kroenkelen' on Car-free Sunday
Wander through the green belt around Bruges by bike or on foot, or stroll through the quiet streets of the city on car-free Sunday (10.00 a.m.-6.00 p.m.).
INFORMATION > www.brugge.be

Zandfeesten (Zand Festival)
Antiques and second-hand market on 't Zand (see above).

14-18: THE WAR IN IMAGES | BRUGES DURING THE GREAT WAR
City Halls (Belfry), 14 October 2014 until 22 February 2015

With three Great War exhibitions at a single location, Bruges goes in search of its own wartime past and seeks to trace the impact – still felt today – of the terrible events that took place between 1914 and 1918. In a historical section, curator Sophie De Schaepdrijver recalls the war years in occupied Bruges through contemporary photographs and images. In a second section, Magnum photographer Carl De Keyzer gives new life to a series of 100-year-old glass negatives, from which he has made new prints, with David Van Reybrouck providing the necessary textual commentaries. In the third exhibition, ten international Magnum photographers reflect on the theme of war – a theme which, sadly enough, is still a current one. Attention will also be devoted to various manifestations that perpetuate the continuing remembrance of the Great War. During the year a number of other interesting events relating to the First World War will be organized in Bruges. You can find more info on www.brugge.be. And visitors who really want to explore the old front region can perhaps take advantage of one of the suggestions made in the chapter 'Excursions from Bruges – In search of the Great War' *(see page 155)*.

October

Jazz Brugge
A four-day festival of top-quality jazz concerts and jam sessions by some of Europe's leading musicians.
INFORMATION > www.jazzbrugge.be

Razor Reel Fantastic Film Festival
Two weeks of fantastic fun for the lovers of fantastic films: from fairylike fantasies to hideous horror – and not just new releases, but also classic 'oldies' and cult masterpieces. In addition to the film showings, there are also workshops, exhibitions and a fantasy film & book fair.
INFORMATION > www.rrfff.be

November

Razor Reel Fantastic Film Festival
A festival for fantastic film fans.
(see above)

December

Christmas Market and ice-rink
For a whole month you can soak up the Christmas atmosphere on the Markt (Market Square) at the Simon Stevinplein; on the Market Square you can even pull on your ice-skates and glide gracefully around the temporary rink in the shadow of the Belfry.

December Dance
A festival of contemporary dance that allows many of today's leading choreographers to strut their stuff and do their thing!
INFORMATION > www.decemberdance.be

Take advantage!

With the Brugge City Card you can enjoy reduced admission to a wide number of events. You'll find all details in the free magazine events@brugge. (For further information, see page 12.)

Tips from Bruges connoisseurs

Working with the best view over Bruges, World Heritage City

Baroque in the air

Frank Deleu, mad about music, knew how to make use of his passion. He is Bruges' carilloneur and he was a producer at Klara, the classical radio broadcasting station. As he is also an enthusiastic bon vivant who likes to wander through the city and her glorious past, it is abundantly clear that he is a unique personality who knows everything about Bruges' immaterial heritage and the history of her most famous tower.

IDENTIKIT

Name: Frank Deleu
Nationality: Belgian
Date of birth: 23 August 1952
Lives in Bruges since 1984.
The city's carilloneur, the man with the loftiest place of work in the historic city centre.

Frank Deleu looks down on Bruges; literally, that is. At least three times a week, the city's carilloneur climbs the three hundred and sixty-six steps of the belfry to reach his place of work. A long, 'uphill' walk that takes him eight minutes (providing visitors don't hold him up) and eventually brings him to his unique percussion instrument. The 47 bells date mainly from the 18th century and have recently been restored. But in spite of his lonely place of work, the city bell ringer is anything but a loner. 'It's just part and parcel of my job to play an instrument high and dry above the crowds. I don't do it for the applause, of course, I wouldn't hear it anyway. It's more of a passion that has grown on me.'

This iconic building – in medieval Flanders the belfries were regarded as a symbol of civic liberty – may have lost its original function of telling local people the time, but the carillon remains immensely popular with natives and visitors alike. In summer the evening recitals attract large crowds to the belfry's courtyard. Others prefer to listen to the sound of the bells at their own favourite spots in the city. The narrow Breidelstraat is one such spot, with its near-perfect acoustics, while listeners on the Burg also sitting on the front row, musically speaking! Many writers have also sung the praises of the carillon of Bruges. Some of them were world-famous, such as Henry Wadsworth Longfellow, Charles Baudelaire and Jules Verne. Le carilloneur de Bruges even inspired three operas. And during the mid-19th century many English visitors came especially to Bruges, then the poorest city in the country, just to listen to the bells.

'Klankentoren'

Each day Frank Deleu is filled with admiration for the beauty that Bruges has managed to preserve, the concentra-

'Not only has Bruges been perfectly preserved in time, the streets are also kept very tidy.'

tion of her museums and art works, her many intimate historical places and her busy cultural agenda. 'Not only has Bruges been perfectly preserved in time, the streets are also kept very tidy. I therefore hope that the city will be able to look after her historical face in the future, Like many of the Italian cities have done: by restricting traffic and keep away contemporary architectural experiments. There is plenty of room for them away from the city centre.'

VIA BRUGENSIS

History is literally to be found on the cobbles of Bruges' streets, that is to say along the forty scallops that form the Bruges section of the Via Brugensis – the ancient pilgrims' route to Santiago de Compostela. The scallops are a modest homage to the thousands of pilgrims that have followed the route from the region of the Zwin via Bruges, Menin and Tournai to Sebourg near Valenciennes in the north of France, where they used to join the GR long-distance footpath.

SUMMERY CARILLON SOUNDS

The visitor who wishes to listen to Frank Deleu from the most advantageous spot should hasten to the courtyard of the Belfry on a Monday or Wednesday evening during the summer months. The recital kicks off at 9.00 p.m. For the next hour the carilloneur will then indulge in his passion for his unique instrument. Deleu also plays the carillon throughout the year from 11.00 to 12.00 a.m. on Wednesday, Saturday and Sunday.

But this does not mean that the city bell ringer is against innovation and modernity. For example, he is very enthusiastic about the Sound Factory, an interactive space for aural art on the panoramic roof of the Concertgebouw (Concert Hall). To celebrate 500 years of the carilloneur's art an inventory was made of all the bells in the historic city centre. The name of the maker and the place of manufacture were established for each bell, following which its own unique sound was recorded. Via two interactive touch screens, visitors can use these sounds to compose their own carillion concert and then listen to it being played over the city.

See page 89 for all practical information on the Sound Factory.

Frank Deleu
Best addresses

FAVOURITE SPOT

» **Onze-Lieve-Vrouw-ter-Potterie**, Potterierei 79B, www.museabrugge. be, closed on Monday

'The most moving place in town is the museum and **church of Our Lady of the Pottery**, a slightly out-of-the way spot, but one that well rewards the effort of finding it. The building is filled to the brim with jewels from a bygone age, from 16ᵗʰ-century household goods to furniture and unique paintings that time seems to have forgotten. An experience that will live long in your memory.'

RESTAURANTS

» **Diligence**, Hoogstraat 5, tel. +32 (0)50 33 16 60, closed on Tuesday and Wednesday

'I am a big fan of the simple and authentic spontaneity of the Diligence. No matter who walks in through the door, the welcome is always warm and friendly, and they are immediately shown to a cosy table in this somewhat dark but always hospitable restaurant. No unnecessary fuss and frills. Just plain and simple Flemish dishes that will leave you wanting more.'

» **Restaurant Pergola**, Meestraat 7, tel. +32 (0)50 44 76 50, www.restaurantpergola.be, closed on Tuesday and Wednesday

'Bruges has many delightful terraces, but the terrace at Restaurant Pergola certainly comes in the top ten. Here, far from the noise of the crowds, you can admire the solemn beauty of the Groenerei, while sampling one of the restaurant's excellent and inventive dishes. Satisfaction guaranteed!'

» **Sint-Joris**, Markt 29, tel. +32 (0)50 33 30 62, www.restaurant-sintjoris.be,
  closed on Tuesday evening (from 5.00 p.m. onwards) and Wednesday

'Some people love top-quality gastronomic fireworks, but I prefer simple and tasty cooking. Such as the delicious everyday dishes you can find in the St. Joris. Its convenient and picturesque location on the Market Square makes it worth the recommendation alone!'

» **Carlito's**, Hoogstraat 21, tel. +32 (0)50 49 00 75, www.carlitos.be,
  no closing day

'Nothing is simpler yet more delicious than a really good pizza. Not too much topping, but just the right amount of day-fresh ingredients. Carlo also makes plenty of great-tasting pasta dishes, but I always go for one of those perfect pizzas. The simple things in life are often the best. Basta!'

» **Trium**, Academiestraat 23, tel. +32 (0)50 33 30 60, www.trattoriatrium.be,
  closed on Monday

'Every visit to Trium is a real experience. As soon as you enter, you think you are in Naples. Complete with gesticulating Italian waiters, who demonstrate all the flare and passion for which their native country is famous! Trium guarantees atmosphere and theatricality by the bucketful, which perfectly complements their honest and authentic pasta.'

CAFÉS

» **Craenenburg**, Markt 16,
  tel. +32 (0)50 33 34 02,
  www.craenenburg.be,
  no closing day

'Craenenburg is the last "real" café on the Market Square. It was from this building that Margaret of York followed the great tournament of 1468. And it was also from here that Maximilian of Austria was forced to watch the torture and execution of his own sheriff and counsellor. Today, it is a favourite spot for local people, where they can catch up on all the latest city gossip and news.'

» **Concertgebouwcafé**, 't Zand 34, tel. +32 (0)50 47 69 81,
  www.concertgebouw.be/café, closed on Sunday, Monday and Tuesday

'The Concertgebouwcafé (at the Concert Hall) is the ideal place to enjoy an after-per-
formance drink and chat. This trendy bar has real star-quality! Enjoy a coffee or some
of their great finger food as you watch the rest of the world pass by outside.'

» **Cultuurcafé Biekorf**, Naaldenstraat 4, tel. +32 (0)499 32 64 78,
  www.ccbrugge.be, closed on Sunday

'You can find this café on the inner courtyard between the city's cultural centre and
the main library. It can be reached via both these buildings, and also from the
Naaldenstraat. Why not give it a try? If you're lucky, you might drop in on one of their
regular surprise acts.'

» **'t Hof van Rembrandt**, Eiermarkt 10, tel. +32 (0)50 33 74 50,
  www.thofvanrembrandt.be, no closing day

''t Hof van Rembrandt is the 'place to be' for real beer-lovers. The café offers a wide selection of the finest beers in Belgium. In summer, you can enjoy the pleasant outdoor
terrace. In winter, you can sip your pint next to the comfort of a blazing open hearth.'

» **'t Klein Venetië**, Braambergstraat 1, tel. +32 (0)475 72 52 25, no closing day

''t Klein Venetië well deserves its name. The café has magnificent views of the city's
canals and the Rozenhoedkaai. This is one of the most photographed locations in
Bruges – so remember to smile!'

SHOPPING LIST

» **Rombaux**, Mallebergplaats 13,
  tel. +32 (0)50 33 25 75,
  www.rombaux.be, closed on
  Sunday and Monday morning
  and public holidays

'This jam-packed music temple has
been promoting classical music, jazz

and top-quality contemporary music in Bruges for three generations. In all that
time, the interior has hardly changed, apart from an occasional lick of paint. There
is no better place to seek expert advice about really good music.'

» **Raaklijn**, Kuipersstraat 1, tel. +32 (0)50 33 67 20,
www.boekhandelraaklijn.be, closed on Sunday

'The Raaklijn Book Store is a home from home for literature fans. It's a place where you can nose around for hours, just enjoying the pleasure of looking for what you want. And usually you will find something to tickle your fancy! You will often find me here.'

» **Callebert**, Wollestraat 25, tel. +32 (0)50 33 50 61, www.callebert.be,
closed on Sunday morning and Monday morning

'A design-lover like me can always find something of interest at Callebert's. Littala glass work, Alessi gadgets, Georg Jensen cutlery, a Stelton wine cooler, a bright pink pouffe from Quinze&Milan or a streamlined chair from Verner Panton: Callebert's has it all – and much more besides! Sometimes I hardly know where to start.'

» **I Love Coffee**, Sint-Jakobsstraat 10, tel. +32 (0)498 51 63 40,
https://www.facebook.com/EspressobarILoveCoffee, closed on Sunday

'This brand new espresso bar not only has a beautiful interior, but also serves delicious coffee. Hardly surprising, since all the coffee beans are roasted on site. If you want to enjoy "the cup that cheers" in the privacy of your own home, you can buy one of the many fragrant, freshly-ground coffee mixes. And, of course, you can always order a take-away coffee. But my favourite option is to take the time to savour a piping-hot espresso in the bar itself.'

» **Cursief**, Baron Ruzettelaan 193, tel. +32 (0)50 35 39 25

'I am not really a great shopper, but if I am looking for old books or second-hand records I like to pop in to Cursief. A pearl that - regrettably - you can only visit by appointment.'

SECRET TIP

» **Concertgebouw**, 't Zand 34 , tel. +32 (0)50 47 69 99, www.concertgebouw.be

'Every year the Concertgebouw (Concert Hall) manages to charm friend and foe alike with its varied programme of the very highest quality. I am particularly looking forward to the annual Bach Academy at the end of January as well as the dozens of other concerts that take place throughout the year. What's more, a visit to the Sound Factory is always great fun, because it allows you to be creative with different noises and sounds. You can experiment as much as you like.'

Flemish Primitives in the spotlight

Till-Holger Borchert sees respect as the key to success

He was born in Hamburg, he lives in Brussels and he thoroughly enjoys his work in Bruges as he finds himself surrounded by six centuries of fine arts, and especially the magnificent masterpieces of the Flemish Primitives. In 2002, Till-Holger Borchert was one of the curators of Bruges, Cultural Capital of Europe. Today he is chief curator of the Groeninge Museum and the Arentshuis.

IDENTIKIT

Name: Till-Holger Borchert
Nationality: German
Date of birth: 4 January 1967
This chief curator of the Groeninge Museum lives in Brussels but works in Bruges. He is the author of countless publications on the Flemish Primitives.

'Bruges is an exceptionally beautiful city,' says Till-Holger Borchert. 'What's more, it is also a wonderfully liveable place, partly because of the clever and careful way in which the city has been able to mix her medieval character with a modern ambiance. As early as the 13th century, the concentration of wealthy citizens enabled Bruges to become the commercial heart of North-western Europe. In the 15th century, the Burgundian authorities took successful structural measures, which resulted in an increase of the population and had a positive effect on the city's further development. Just as importantly, Bruges was spared of the any ravages of the so-called Iconoclastic Fury, which caused so much damage in other cities. That spirit of respect and tolerance still pervades the city today. I must say it is a great joy to be here. The countless locals and visitors will surely fully agree with me.'

Madonnas from around the Corner

'Nearly every day I go and greet two masterpieces: Jan van Eyck's *Madonna*

'Nearly every day I go and greet two masterpieces.'

with Canon Joris van der Paele at the Groeninge Museum and Hans Memling's *Madonna and Maarten van Nieuwenhove* at the Saint John's Hospital. I am not saying that I discover something new every time I look at them, but my curiosity and my pleasure remain as great as ever. And I still try and find out new things about them. They just continue to fascinate me! I sometimes wonder why people from all corners of the world have always found the Flemish Primitives so absorbing. The answer perhaps lies in the fact that for the very first time in art history we are confronted with recognisable people and familiar objects that correspond to today's reality. Even a Madonna seems to look like the woman from around the corner. The Flemish Primitives laid the foundation of an artistic concept that in its realism is perfectly recognisable and therefore understandable to a modern-day observer. The Flemish Primitives discovered the individual. Quite a feat. Those Flemish painters were also dab hands at solving the problems. They explored space in an incredibly skilful and sophisticated way,

INTERESTING TOMBS

'The tomb of Charles the Bold isn't the only attraction of the Church of Our Lady. Mary of Burgundy, Charles' daughter and only child, lies buried in its crypt. She was barely twenty-five years old when she died after falling from her horse when hawking. The face on her coffin was modelled after her death mask. The metal casket with the heart of her son Philip the Fair is exhibited in the choir aisle.'

🏛 MUSEUM SHOP

'Whoever enters the museum shop of the Groeninge Museum will leave with some wonderful memories, that I can assure you. Perhaps you will take home your favourite art treasures in the shape of a handsomely illustrated book or a reproduction on a poster maybe, or depicted on a few picture postcards. And why don't you surprise yourself with an original souvenir? I have caught not only some of my delighted fellow curators buying just such a present for themselves, but my wife as well!'

for example by placing a mirror somewhere in the room. In Memling's diptych, a round mirror on the left-hand side behind the Madonna reflects the interior she is sitting in. In it, her own silhouette is painted just a whisker away from the silhouette of the patrician Maarten van Nieuwenhove, Memling's patron. Truly magnificent. Are these works of art still capable of moving me?

Absolutely. For pure emotion a painter like Rogier van der Weyden touches me more deeply than Jan van Eyck. The works of Van Eyck or Memling impress me more with their intellectual and conceptual qualities. Van der Weyden and Van Eyck: it is worth visiting the treasure houses of Bruges, even if only for the pleasure of enjoying these two opposite ends of artistic spectrum.'

Till-Holger Borchert
Best addresses

FAVOURITE SPOT

» **The churches of Bruges**
'The great churches of Bruges possess wonderful art collections, containing pieces that wouldn't disgrace any top-flight museum. Don't forget to look up at the tower of the Church of Our Lady. It is, with its 122 metres, the second tallest brick church-building in the world. When in Saint Saviour's, do go and marvel at the frescoes in the baptistery. And Saint James' Church is worth its while for the impressive **mausoleum of the De Gros family**, because this sculptural masterpiece reveals par excellence the self-confidence and power of the Burgundian elite.'

RESTAURANTS

» **Den Amand**, Sint-Amandsstraat 4, tel. +32 (0)50 34 01 22, www.denamand.be, closed on Sunday and Wednesday evening
'In Den Amand I once saw a German restaurant critic copy out the entire menu card. You can't get higher praise than that! A small and elegant bistro, where you will find both tourists and local people enjoying the excellent food.'

» **Rock Fort**, Langestraat 15, tel. +32 (0)50 33 41 13, www.rock-fort.be, closed on Saturday and Sunday
"Rock Fort serves original, contemporary dishes with a modern twist. It's cooking is so good that the place is packed all week long. Local people love it, and I also like to pop in from time to time. But be careful: it is closed during the weekends.'

» **'t Schrijverke**, Gruuthusestraat 4, tel. +32 (0)50 33 29 08,
www.tschrijverke.be, closed on Monday

'This homely restaurant is named after a poem by Guido Gezelle, which hangs in a place of honour next to the door. But 't Schrijverke is above all rightly famed for its delicious regional dishes and its "Karmeliet" beer on tap.'

» **Tanuki**, Oude Gentweg 1, tel. +32 (0)50 34 75 12, www.tanuki.be,
closed on Monday and Tuesday

'A little piece of Japan in the heart of Bruges. A true temple of food, where you immediately drop your voice to the level of a whisper, so that you don't disturb the silent enjoyment of the other diners. In the open kitchen the chef does magical things with sushi and sashimi, and prepares his seven course menus with true oriental serenity.'

» **Den Gouden Harynck**, Groeninge 25, tel. +32 (0)50 33 76 37,
www.dengoudenharynck.be, closed on Sunday and Monday

'Den Gouden Harynck is a household name in Bruges, known and loved by foodies of all kinds. It is also one of the most pleasant star-rated restaurants in the city – as anyone who has ever been there will tell you.'

CAFÉS

» **Delaney's Irish Pub & Restaurant**,
Burg 8, tel. +32 (0)50 34 91 45,
www.delaneys.be, no closing day,
but closed every morning (until 12.00
noon) and also in the afternoon from
Monday to Friday (between 3.00 p.m.
and 6.00 p.m.)

'It's always party time in this Irish pub, with its distinctive international atmosphere. Delaney's is the kind of place where you can rub shoulders with the whole world at the bar.'

» **The Druid's Cellar**, Sint-Amandsstraat 11, tel. +32 (0)50 61 41 44,
www.thedruidscellar.eu, closed on Monday and every morning until 11.00 a.m.

'I like to drop in at The Druid's Cellar every now and again, even if only to watch Drew, my favourite barkeeper, in action. Or simply to relax and enjoy a glass from their wide range of Scottish and Irish whiskies. They always taste just that little bit better in The Druids.'

» **Café Marcel**, Niklaas Desparsstraat 7-9, tel. +32 (0)50 33 55 02,
www.hotelmarcel.be, no closing day

'You can find this brand new café right in the heart of the city centre. Café Marcel is Bruges' refined version of a contemporary vintage café. In other words, a café from the days of yesteryear, but in tight, new design setting. Think of dark wooden floor-boards, simple lamps, leather benches and original wood panelling. You can pop in here for a tasty breakfast or an aperitif with tapas. A welcome new discovery!'

» **Den Express**, Stationsplein, tel. +32 (0)50 38 88 85,
www.horeca-station-brugge.be, no closing day

'The Den Express station bar is ideal for people like me, who travel a lot. Here I can enjoy a quiet coffee before setting off on my journey, safe from all the hustle and bustle going on outside.'

» **Hollandse Vismijn**, Vismarkt 4, tel. +32 (0)50 33 33 01, closed on Tuesday

'Whenever I fancy one of the popular Belgian beers, you will probably find me in the Hollandse Vismijn. This cheap and cheerful 'people's pub' is on the Fish Market. It is the type of café where everybody knows everybody and where you always get a warm welcome. Cheers!'

SHOPPING LIST

» **Antiquariaat Van de Wiele**, Sint-Salvatorskerkhof 7, tel. +32 (0)50 33 63 17,
www.marcvandewiele.com, closed on Tuesday, Wednesday and Sunday

'For art and history I was fortunate enough to discover Marc Van de Wiele Antiques. This is undoubtedly one of the best addresses in a city that is rich in antique shops. The place to find unique, illustrated books from days long gone by.'

» **Boekhandel De Reyghere**, Markt 12, tel. +32 (0)50 33 34 03,
www.dereyghere.be, closed on Sunday

'For all my other reading material I rely on De Reyghere, conveniently located on the Market Square. Foreign visitors feel instantly at home in this book and newspaper store, primarily because of the large number of international titles it has on sale.'

» **Den Gouden Karpel**, Vismarkt 9-10-11, tel. +32 (0)50 33 33 89,
www.dengoudenkarpel.be, closed on Sunday and Monday

'The fishing family Ameloot have been running Den Gouden Karpel with heart and soul for many years. It is not only an excellent fish shop with an equally excellent catering service, but is also a really great fish bar. If you don't want the bother of making your own fish dish at home, in the bar you can sample oysters (European or Japanese), winkles, whelks, Zeebrugge fish soup, crab claws, half lobsters, fresh-salmon quiche, shrimp croquettes, etc. For a fish-lover like myself, it is hard to walk past Den Gouden Karpel without stopping to buy something.'

» **Deldycke Delicatessen**, Wollestraat 23, tel. +32 (0)50 33 43 35,
www.deldycke.be, closed on Tuesday

'In the 15th century the Spaniard Pedro Tafur was already praising Bruges for its wide available selection of exotic fruits and rare spices. The Deldycke Delicatessen is proud to continue this centuries-old tradition. Here, all your culinary wishes will be fulfilled.'

» **Kleding Parallax**, Zuidzandstraat 17, tel. +32 (0)50 33 23 02,
www.parallax.be, closed on Sunday morning (in January, February,
July and August: whole Sunday) and public holidays

'I always buy my socks at Parallax, but they are also experts at stylishly camouflaging my beer belly! Highly recommended for other fashion victims and the vestimentally challenged! Boss, Scabal, Zilton, Falke: you can find them all here.'

SECRET TIP

» **Museumshop**, Arentshof,
Dijver 16, www.museabrugge.be,
closed on Monday

» **Gezelle Museum, Jerusalem
Chapel and Lace Centre, Our
Lady of the Pottery** and **Folklore
Museum:** info on pages 81, 84, 86 and 90

'Whenever I want to take a breather, I saunter down Saint Anne's, Bruges' most striking working-class neighbourhood. You can still sense the charm of an authentic community in the streets around the Folklore Museum. It goes without saying that it is very peaceful there at night, a very rare occurrence in a city like Bruges. The area boasts many fascinating places, too. Off the cuff, if I may: Our Lady of the Pottery, the Lace Centre, medieval **Jerusalem Chapel** and the Gezelle Museum.'

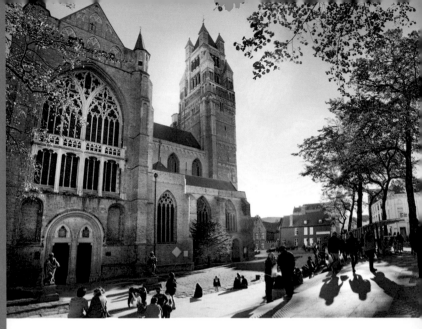

A varied cultural palette

Brody Neuenschwander, an American in Bruges

Looking back it seemed almost inevitable that the world-famous calligrapher, Brody Neuenschwander, would one day end up in Bruges. It was his love for the Flemish Primitives (and his wife, of course!) that first pushed him in this direction. His medieval house, with its 14th century mural paintings, will ensure that he now stays for good. The story of a Texan with a Bruges heart.

IDENTIKIT

Name: Brody Neuenschwander
Nationality: American
Date of birth: 8 September 1958
Has been living in Bruges since 1993. World-renowned calligraphist, whose important commissions include work for the American, British and Belgian governments, as well as the BBC and the Royal Mail; a man who stands with one foot in the medieval past of Bruges and the other foot firmly in the future.

Brody Neuenschwander might well have been born and bred in the wide-open spaces of Houston, Texas, but he has always belonged in Bruges. He was a part of the city and the city was a part of him. When, as an art student in distant America, he first learnt about the Flemish Primitives, he immediately jumped on a plane and came to see for himself. And he was impressed by what he found. 'I was just 20. I stood on the Bonifacius Bridge and looked around me: "Wow!" I thought, "This is a really great city".'

At that time, he never dreamed that he might one day live here. The years passed. Brody studied many of the medieval breviaries produced in Bruges. 'These are richly illustrated medieval manuscripts that the well-to-do classes had made for "use" during the hours of divine office, the eight moments each day when Christians were supposed to pray. From the 11th to the 14th century, many manuscripts of this kind were crafted and exported from Bruges,' says Brody. When his grandmother bequeathed him a substantial sum of money, he immediately went out and bought one of his own. 'This was my own little piece of medieval treasure, a thing of rare beauty.'

rooms, the do-it-yourselfer suddenly cried out in amazement. 'At first, my wife thought that I had fallen off the ladder, but in fact I had discovered a medieval mural painting, hidden way for centuries beneath layers of plaster and paint. And it wasn't just a rough design sketch but a completed work, which now ranks as one of the most important wall paintings of its kind in Flanders.' But Brody keeps a sense of perspective. 'I guess I just exchanged one work of art for another. And yes, it's fun to think that I was somehow destined to live here, in this house.'

It was only later in London that he first met his wife-to-be – a local girl from Bruges. It was clear from the start that the newly married couple would make their home in her native city. So the breviary was sold and exchanged for a beautiful house fronting onto one of the city's many canals. It later transpired that this was the oldest house in what had once been the medieval harbour quarter. While he was renovating one of the

Bruges: the world centre for Western calligraphy

Although the world-famous calligrapher could now live anywhere in the world he wants to, he remains faithful to his adopted hometown. 'Here, there is a new treat for your eyes, almost every day of the year. And no matter where you go and what you see, it is always better in Bruges.

'I stood on the Bonifacius Bridge and looked around me:
"Wow!" I thought, "this is a really great city".'

GENETIC HERITAGE

'Texas is a land of wide-open spaces. Everything is big. The houses, the landscape, the restaurant tables... Here, the scale of everything is different. In Bruges you only have to dig a hole in your back garden to stumble across the past. First a tile, then a bit of sand, then another tile, next a brick... The different layers of history run so deep and are so close together that things evolve more slowly here. An American will sometimes change his mind overnight. Someone from Bruges will not.'

What's more, the city is now the centre of Western calligraphy. There is no other place in Europe or America that even comes close. Bruges not only has a great number of professional calligraphists, but also several calligraphy shops and a wide range of calligraphy courses. And we are not standing still. We are constantly active, seeking to bring the past and the present together in new creative ways. In Bruges, innovation always stimulates some kind of dialogue with the past, and

that is what I find so interesting.'
If an artist elsewhere in the world or one of Neuenschwander's important 'customers' (the American, British and Belgian governments, the BBC, etc.) need a top-quality calligrapher, they just pick up the phone and call Brody. One week he will be working for director Peter Greenaway, the next week on a documentary series for the BBC, and the week after that on some project of his own. Sitting still – and doing nothing – is not an option.

Brody Neuenschwander
Best addresses

FAVOURITE SPOT

» **The attics of the Sint-Janshospi-
taal (St. John's Hospital)**, Mariastraat 38, www.museabrugge.be,
closed on Monday

'In these **attics**, you can hear and feel the
silence. It is as if time has stood still. With
the huge beams, massive wooden pillars and the small surface of medieval tiled floor,
it is easy to imagine yourself back in the 14th century.'

RESTAURANTS

» **Books and Brunch**, Garenmarkt 30,
tel. +32 (0)50 70 90 79, www.
booksandbrunch.be, closed
on Monday, Sunday and public
holidays

'Books and Brunch is a unique and very
welcome addition to the food scene in
Bruges. A delightful breakfast, coffee and lunch address, where you can pick up a
book or two, or simply enjoy a good read while you are waiting for your delicious
homemade cake or perfect cappuccino. And the kids will also find something to
keep them amused in the mini-library.'

» **De Lotus**, Wapenmakersstraat 5, tel. +32 (0)50 33 10 78, www.lotus-brugge.be,
only open at noon (11.45 a.m. to 14.00 p.m.), closed on Saturday and Sunday

'This vegetarian lunch restaurant is now a Bruges classic. For the past 20 years it has
been offering tasty vegetarian dishes in its sober yet refined décor. Simple wooden
stools and chairs, and everything served on their attractive ceramic tableware.
Solo eaters can flick through one of the many available papers and magazines.'

» **Lieven**, Philipstockstraat 45, tel. +32 (0)50 68 09 75, www.etenbijlieven.be, closed on Sunday and Monday

'In just a short time the stylish Lieven has grown into a trendy success restaurant. The menu is limited: just four starters and four main courses. But the food is exceptionally refined, in a contemporary interior with character.'

» **A'Qi**, Gistelse Steenweg 686, 8200 Sint-Andries, tel. +32 (0)50 30 05 99, www.restaurantaqi.be, closed on Sunday evening, Monday and Tuesday

'A'Qi means something like 'life force' and that is exactly what this quality restaurant wants to offer. Each new visit is a total experience that nourishes both body and mind. Based on the classic traditions of Flemish cooking, but enriched with flashes of foreign inspiration.'

» **Cafedraal**, ZIlverstraat 38, tel. +32 (0)50 34 08 45, www.cafedraal.be, closed on Sunday

'This 15th century building has an enchanting enclosed garden, which you can enjoy from the first sun of spring until deep into the autumn. The specialities of the house are the classic meat and fish dishes for which Flanders is famous.'

CAFÉS

» **One**, Arsenaalstraat 55, tel. +32 (0)50 33 80 88, www.one-minnewater.be closed on Monday

'One of the most beautiful terraces in Bruges, hidden away in one of the city's most romantic parks. The ideal place to enjoy a quiet aperitif, some tapas or a coffee and a cake. And all in an elegant setting that cheers the heart and pleases the eye.'

» **De Garre**, De Garre 1, tel. +32 (0)50 34 10 29, www.degarre.be, no closing day but closed every morning (until 12.00 a.m.) and on Saturday (until 11.00 a.m.)

'You can find this authentic 'beer' cafe in one of the smallest streets in Bruges. Here you can choose from no fewer than 130 different beers, ranging from regional brews and commercial beers on tap to bottled abbey ales. Some are well-known, some are not so well-known – but they are all well worth a try. Cheers!'

» **Bar of Grand Hotel Casselbergh,** Hoogstraat 6, tel. +32 (0)50 44 65 00,
www.grandhotelcasselbergh.com, closed every morning (until 12.00 a.m.)
'This glorious four-star hotel has a bar that is as magnificent as it is charming. High
ceilings, luxurious wall hangings, dazzling chandeliers, a splendid open hearth and a
wide selection of quality drinks, with *premium brands* from both home and abroad.'

SHOPPING LIST

» **Symposion,** Oostmeers 41,
tel. +32 (0)50 33 61 31,
www.symposion.be,
closed on Sunday and Monday

'A writer's paradise, where calligraphic
soul mates can commune with each
other. Here you can not only find
everything a calligrapher needs, but
there is also a quiet place to read and a
fine section of carefully crafted gifts and knick-knacks. From calligraphed kitchen
aprons through framed silk-screen prints to modest but original postcards.'

» **Atelier Maud Bekaert,** Sint-Clarastraat 40, tel. +32 (0)50 34 70 05,
www.lettersinsteen.be, open on Friday and Saturday morning
'It was poetry that first led Maud Bekaert to take up the art of letter-cutting. Today
she engraves her own poetry in letters of stone and several of her creations can be
seen here and there in the streets of Bruges. Her small but atmospheric workshop
is the place for souvenirs with character.'

» **simBOLik,** Katelijnestraat 139 , tel. +32 (0)495 30 70 56, www.simbolik.be,
closed Sunday to Wednesday
'Calligraphers can enjoy themselves to their hearts content every Thursday, Friday
and Saturday in this open workshop. And every first Sunday of the month a poet,
theatre-maker or musician is invited to come and 'do his creative thing'. In short, a
place where creative souls can come into contact with each other in comfortable
and informal surroundings.'

» **De Kringloopwinkel**, Langestraat 169-171, tel. +32 (0)50 34 94 00,
www.klctrad.be, closed on Sunday and Monday

'This is where true creativity begins. For next to nothing you can pick up all kinds of interesting things in this second-hand store. Some are just useful; others might be a source of artistic inspiration. Who knows? From vintage handbags through porcelain objects to full dinner services! Well worth a look.'

» **De Andere Kijk**, Garenmarkt 28, tel. +32 (0)50 34 21 61,
closed on Monday and Tuesday

'*You name it, we frame it* is the slogan of this workshop, where you can indeed frame all your artistic and other treasures, whatever their shape and size.'

SECRET TIP

» **The Sint-Gillis (St. Giles') district**

'A popular, working-class area, with street after street of small workers' houses, dominated by a magnificent church and the memory of a mysterious cemetery, now long since disappeared, where (amongst others) Hans Memling was buried. That, in a nutshell, is the St. Giles' Quarter. This was, indeed, the neighbourhood where Memling lived and worked. In 1480 he bought a house in the Sint-Jorisstraat and a few years later he also bought the adjoining property, 'Den Ingel'. Both buildings were demolished in the 19th century.

There is now a plaque marking the site, which reminds people of the life and work of this great Flemish Primitive. There is a second such plaque in the **St. Giles' Church**, where he was buried in 1494. While you are searching to find these plaques, don't forget to admire the fine combination of the Gothic and Neo-Gothic styles in St. Giles'. In particular, the quarter offers an opportunity to stop and admire the often underrated qualities of the Neo-Gothic period. This was the last real crafts movement in Western architecture, which played a not insignificant role in shaping the Bruges that we can still see today.'

100 years after the Great War

Sharon Evans, in search of the First World War

Just a handful of kilometres from Bruges lies the Westhoek region. This green and pleasant land is now a haven of peace, but precisely one hundred years ago, between 1914 and 1918, it was the setting for some of the most terrible fighting the world has ever seen. It was the Westhoek that first brought Sharon Evans to Belgium many years ago. Nowadays, this Bruges 'settler' leads visitors on tours of the old battlefields.

IDENTIKIT

Name: Sharon Evans
Nationality: Australian
Date of birth: 9 September 1965
Lives in Bruges since 1991. Sharon runs Quasimodo and organises bus trips to the Westhoek, where she gives guided tours to many hundreds of tourists.

Sharon was born in Asia, as the daughter of a serving Australian soldier. Having moved from place to place in that part of the world several times during her formative years, she eventually decided that the time had come to see what things were like on the other side of the planet! A year later, her wanderlust had still not been satisfied, and so she decided to 'hang around for a bit longer' in Europe. The choice was between Bruges and Vienna. 'I felt that Bruges was smaller, prettier, cleaner and friendlier – and so I chose Flanders.' Today, many years later, this citizen of the world still lives and works in Bruges. Her very first visit to Belgium – and the reason why she was so determined to come to our little country – took Sharon to the Westhoek. This was the place where her great-grandfather, together with his many comrades, had fought side by side during the Great War.

'In the Westhoek I had the feeling that I was following in my great-grandfather's footsteps. Here in Flanders, I discovered a piece of my own history.'

14-18: THE WAR IN IMAGES | BRUGES IN THE GREAT WAR

Bruges commemorates the Great War with three exhibitions at a single location. A historical section with photographs, posters, portraits and uniforms tells the story of Bruges during the war. The curator is Sophie De Schaepdrijver. In a second exhibition, Magnum photographer Carl De Keyzer shows a selection of original photographs illustrating aspects of the First World War, selected with a contemporary view in mind and with explanatory texts by David Van Reybrouck. In the third exhibition, ten other international Magnum photographers show their own work on the theme of war, reflecting on this sad subject in their own manner and from their own perspective.
City Halls (Belfry), 14 October 2014 to 22 February 2015

BRUGES, OCCUPIED CITY

Less well-known – because the history of the Great War mainly focuses on places at the front – is the fact that during the First World War Bruges was the German headquarters for operations on the Atlantic coast. Shortly after the German Marine Infantry had installed their occupation regime in the city, the German High Command decided to convert the harbour at Zeebrugge into a base for their submarine fleet. Bruges also served as a place of relaxation for the German Army and - for the officers, at least - as a place of culture. After serving at the front for a period of 3 to 6 months, German soldiers were allowed a stay of 2 to 4 weeks in Bruges, to rest and recuperate.

If you want to see and experience for yourself the places where the Great War was fought one hundred years ago, you need to travel to the Westhoek. You can find a number of suggestions in the chapter 'Excursions from Bruges – In search of the Great War' *(see page 155)*.

'I am the daughter of a soldier, so I already knew quite a lot about the First World War. And I have always been interested in history; I guess it's just built into my genes! Besides, the Great War was very important for the Australian people. It's true that we lost many of our finest sons, but out of that suffering we discovered our identity as a nation.'

The fascinating Westhoek

On her very first day in Belgium, Sharon immediately set off for the Westhoek. 'It's

BRUGES AND THE GREAT WAR

In the course of 2014, there will be numerous events relating to the First World War on the Bruges cultural agenda. You can find more information and a full summary on www.brugge.be.

a wonderful place, with an undulating and easy-going landscape.' It was also an emotional place for Sharon. 'I had the feeling that I was following in my great-grandfather's footsteps. Walking where he had walked, remembering how he had struggled and fought here all those years ago... It was a really moving and deeply personal experience. Here in Flanders, I discovered a piece of my own history. People who have never been here before find it hard to imagine that this delightful countryside was once a terrible battlefield, full of misery and death. In Tyne Cot Cemetery, the largest British military cemetery on the European mainland, there is a huge memorial wall engraved with the names of 35,000 soldiers who went 'missing', whose bodies were never found. 35,000! Something like that cannot fail to touch you. In the meantime, I have been back to the Westhoek thousands of times, but I will never

THE RAID ON ZEEBRUGGE

During the First World War, Zeebrugge – the outport of Bruges – was transformed into a highly sophisticated submarine base, with the intention of cutting off the overseas supply lines to England. As a result, the British decided to attack the harbour. On 23 April 1918, St. George's Day, a flotilla under Vice-Admiral Keyes made an attempt to block the entrance to the harbour, so that the German U-boats could cause no further damage. This famous raid, one of the most high-risk operations during the entire war, is still commemorated each year.

forget that very first time. And no matter how often I come, it never ceases to make an impression. It's that kind of place; it gets under your skin...'

In 1991 Sharon founded the forerunner of Quasimodo. Originally, she offered her tourist customers both cycling and bus tours, but she eventually decided to concentrate on the latter. Today she runs Quasimodo with her husband, Philippe. The couple have two tours: *WWI Flanders Fields Tour* and *Triple Treat: the best of Belgium in one day*. You can find more info on www.quasimodo.be and on pages 147-148 and 155.

Sharon Evans

Best addresses

FAVOURITE SPOT

» **The canals around Bruges**

'As soon as you leave the city, you find yourself in another world: a green paradise. Whoever follows the Bruges-Ghent Canal or the **Damse Vaart** (Damme Canal), exploring the region by bike, is treated to one picture-postcard scene after another. Not to be missed!'

RESTAURANTS

» **Heer Halewijn**, Walplein 10, tel. +32 (0)50 33 92 61, closed on Monday, Tuesday and during the day (until 6.30 p.m.)

'Heer Halewijn shines brightly on the beautiful Walplein square, which is one of the city's less well-known jewels. You shouldn't expect any gastronomic hocus-pocus here, just good, honest grilled dishes, accompanied by a fine selection of top-quality wines.'

» **Taj Mahal**, Philipstockstraat 6, tel. +32 (0)487 14 74 86 and +32 (0)50 34 22 42, www.tajmahalrestaurant.be, closed on Monday

'I was born in Asia, so of course I like piquant Asian food. And fortunately you can find this in Bruges. I like to order my Indian curries from the Taj Mahal. Hot and spicy!'

» **Narai Thai**, Smedenstraat 43, tel. +32 (0)50 68 02 56,
www.naraithai.be, no closing day

'The Narai Thai is another culinary hot spot: both literally and figuratively! Here you can enjoy dishes ranging from the mildly spicy to punishingly peppery, and all set in a trendy lounge atmosphere. It's almost like being transported to the other side of the world, even if only for an hour or so.'

» **De Vlaamsche Pot**, Helmstraat 3-5, tel. +32 (0)50 34 00 86,
www.devlaamschepot.be, closed on Monday and Tuesday

'Eccentric, yet at the same time very traditionally Flemish. This sounds like a contradiction but the Vlaamsche Pot somehow manages to blend these two extremes together. In this somewhat unusual setting you can enjoy fish stew (*waterzooi*), meat stew (*karbonaden*) and mussels with chips. In other words, the better Flemish classics.'

» **In 't Nieuw Museum**, Hooistraat 42, tel. +32 (0)50 33 12 80,
www.nieuw-museum.com, closed on Wednesday

'Carnivores will just love in 't Nieuw Museum, where delicious hunks of meat are cooked over a charcoal grill. From spare ribs to best end of neck to prime steak. And all in a delightfully relaxed atmosphere. Perfect for families.'

CAFÉS

» **Lokkedize**, Korte Vulderstraat 33,
tel. +32 (0)50 33 44 50, www.lokkedize.
be, closed on Monday, Tuesday and
during the day (until 6.00 p.m.)

'One of my very favourite places. A pleasant bar where you can always enjoy some rhythm & blues, a bit of rock 'n roll or a classic chanson. There are regular live performances and the kitchen stays open really late.'

» **Bistro Du Phare**, Sasplein 2, tel. +32 (0)50 34 35 90, www.duphare.be,
closed on Tuesday and every morning (until 11.00 a.m.)

'Bistro Du Phare is one of those increasingly rare addresses where you can nearly always find live music. A place to be savoured: great on the outside terrace (overlooking the water) in the summer, and cosy inside during the winter.'

» **'t Stokershuis**, Langestraat 7, tel. +32 (0)50 33 55 88,
closed on Tuesday and Wednesday

'Small is beautiful: that could easily be the motto of 't Stokershuis. A traditional city bar in mini-format, with bags of atmosphere. A place you'll find really hard to leave!'

» **Bistro Zwart Huis**, Kuipersstraat 23, tel. +32 (0)50 69 11 40,
www.bistrozwarthuis.be, closed on Monday and Tuesday

'This protected monument was built in 1642 and the facade and the medieval bar-room are truly impressive. Since recently, you can enjoy a bite to eat, a glass of something pleasant and occasional live music.'

» **Café Rose Red**, Cordoeaniersstraat 16, tel. +32 (0)50 33 90 51,
www.cordoeanier.be, no closing day, but closed every morning
(until 11.00 a.m.)

'This slightly out-of-the-way café is specialised in abbey beers and sells a good se-lection of the world's very best 'trappist' brews, which you can either drink in the pleasing interior or in the equally charming courtyard. And if you sample one trap-pist too many, you can always spend the night at the hotel next door, run by the same people!'

SHOPPING LIST

» **Jofre**, Vlamingstraat 7, tel. +32 (0)50 33 39 60, www.jofre.eu,
closed on Sunday

'Admittedly, this ladies clothing boutique is not the cheapest in town, but it has an excellent selection of timeless designs that are well worth the investment. The kind of shop that a woman could spend quite some time in!'

» **De Kaasbolle**, Smedenstraat 11, tel. +32 (0)50 33 71 54, www.dekaasbolle.be,
closed on Wednesday and Sunday afternoon

'Whoever likes a delicious piece of beautifully matured cheese should definitely make their way to De Kaasbolle. From creamy Lucullus, the house cheese, through Tartarin Cognac (a fresh cow's milk cheese with Turkish raisins, marinated in French brandy) to the authentic Greek feta marinade: every one is a real treat for your taste buds.'

» **Da Vinci**, Geldmuntstraat 34, tel. +32 (0)50 33 36 50, https:// www.facebook. com/davincibrugge, open from 14/2 t/m 31/10, no closing day

'Whether it is freezing cold or tropically warm, there are always tourists and local people patiently queuing up outside this deservedly well-known ice-cream parlour. The number of different flavours is almost limitless, and everything – from the ice-cream itself to the sauces – is made on the premises.'

» **Chocolatier Dumon**, Eiermarkt 6, Walstraat 6 and Simon Stevinplein 11, tel. +32 (0)50 22 16 22, www.chocolatierdumon.be, no closing day

'I have been a big fan of Dumon's traditionally-made, top-quality chocolate for years. The Bruges story of confectioner Stephan Dumon began in 1996 on the Eiermarkt. In the meantime, he has also opened a sales point in the Walstraat and an imposing shop on the Simon Stevinplein, where on Saturdays you can even follow chocolate-making demonstrations. But I remain faithful to his small and welcoming shop on the Eiermarkt, where the old saying "good things come in small packages" really applies!'

» **Shoerecrafting**, Langestraat 13, tel. +32 (0)50 33 81 01, www.shoerecrafting.be, **closed on Sunday and Monday**

'Luc Decuyper learnt the cobbler's art at Delvaux and other famous names in the leather trade, and is the man I can always rely on when my shoes start showing signs of wear. This excellent craftsman obviously loves his work - and it really shows in the end result.'

SECRET TIP

» **City Theatre**, Vlamingstraat 29, tel. +32 (0)50 44 30 60, www.ccbrugge.be

'For me, taking in a concert at the City Theatre (Stadschouwburg) is a real treat. Bruges **Royal City Theatre**, in the very heart of the old city, dates from 1870 and is an architectural masterpiece. Every time I visit, I never fail to enjoy the waves of red and gold in the palatial auditorium and the opulent splendour of the majestic foyer. Little wonder that the Bruges theatre is regarded as one of the best preserved city theatres in all Europe.'

Bruges, culinary centre

Bob Eck, a New York foodie living for the day in Bruges

A New Yorker who swaps The Big Apple for the Market Square in Bruges: it sounds like it must be a joke – but that is precisely what Bob Eck, an international manager, did. In his search for a more relaxed style of life, he crossed the Atlantic and set up shop in Flanders. That his new home could satisfy his love for great food was just an added bonus. A conversation with a Dutch-speaking New Yorker.

IDENTIKIT

Name: Bob Eck
Nationality: American
Date of birth: 3 June 1963
Has been living in Bruges since 2011.
Bob Eck is a self-employed marketing consultant
and dedicated foodie.

For many years, Bob Eck led a hundred mile-an-hour existence in the hustle and bustle of New York. He worked long days followed by long nights in the vibrant after-hours social scene of one of the world's greatest cities. It was only when he finally got back to his apartment – usually in the early hours of the morning – that he was able to relax and unwind. But he found himself dreaming increasingly of a different kind of existence, a more 'human' way of life. 'I wanted to live more and work less. I wanted balance. But I couldn't find it. I was still working much more than I was living. In fact, work was my life, it was all I was doing.' The fact that he and his partner were

WELCOME TO THE GASTRONOMIC MECCA OF EUROPE

'Even before we moved to Bruges, I already knew that you can eat here very well – very well indeed. There is no city in the world that has more Michelin stars per 117,000 inhabitants than Bruges.'

In the section 'Restaurants of distinction' (see page 24) you can read which local restaurants offer star quality cooking, which ones have been awarded the Bib Gourmand label and which ones can boast a nice score in the GaultMillau guide. They are numbers that will tickle the palette and the imagination of every hungry gourmet!

unable to marry in New York – something they later did in Connecticut – simply strengthened his urge to leave. The pair decided to move home – not just to a new town or a new state, but to a new country – Belgium, 'a country that clearly promotes tolerance'. His eye immediately settled on the mondaine, worldly city of Bruges. 'Bruges is a beautiful city where you can relax and find peace with yourself. The quality of life is so much higher here than in New York, and thanks

A VALHALLA FOR FOODIES

'Nothing is so much fun as running your errands at the market. And in Bruges you can do that almost every day of the week. I always buy my fresh fish at the delightful old fish market. And I get my fruit, vegetables and flowers every Wednesday, when dozens of stalls take over the Market Square for the morning. Or on Saturday, when there are markets on both 't Zand and the Beursplein. And if I discover that I have forgotten something for the weekend, I can always nip down to the atmospheric Sunday market in Sint-Michiels. So there's choice enough!' (Also see page 35)

*'Here people still take the time to cook properly;
and wherever you go it's just so easy to find really fantastic ingredients.'*

to the fantastic food and wine culture there is always plenty to enjoy. What's more, the pace of living is healthier in Bruges than in Manhattan. Here you have more time for your family, your friends and for good eating! This makes Bruges more relaxed, more open, friendlier. Here people still take the time to cook properly; and wherever you go it's just so easy to find really fantastic ingredients. All this means that, for me, Bruges is like a fairy-tale come true, a city that combines medieval charm with modern, high-tech comfort.'

Hours of dining fun

Even visiting a restaurant is more relaxed on this side of the ocean. 'In New York everything has to go fast. Each restaurant does two or three shifts each evening. Enjoying a nice chat after you meal is simply not done – they want you out as quickly as possible. In Bruges the focus is on what I call 'slow enjoyment'. You start your meal at around eight in the evening and it is only three or four hours later that you finally head for home. In this country, dining out is not only about what you get on your plate (although that's usually pretty damned good); it's about the whole experience.

Restaurateurs are not bothered about turning shift after shift; they are happy if they can send their customers home satisfied at the end of the evening. Because satisfied customers will keep on coming back for more. In my opinion, it's a much smarter approach. I had expected to find a better quality of life in Flanders, but each day my expectations are surpassed – big time! I am thinking, for example, of all that wonderful Bruges chocolate. It's not without good reason that Bruges is rightly called the capital of chocolate. And as for all those top-quality beers, with the city's own beer, 'Brugse Zot', leading the way… Yep, life here is really great!'

A CELEBRATION OF FOOD AND DRINK

'The people of Bruges do full justice to their "Burgundian" reputation as lovers of good food and drink. This reputation will once again be confirmed by the annual Bruges Beer Festival, which this year will be organized is the Beurshalle (Exhibition Hall). Find out what it's like to be a real Burgundian by sampling the many famous Belgian and Bruges beers on offer. Highly recommended!'
(You can find a detailed events calendar on the website www.brugge.be)

Bob Eck
Best addresses

FAVOURITE SPOT

» **Mini-escape behind the cathedral**
'There is a small park behind the
St. Saviour's Cathedral: just a handful
of benches and a small plot of grass,
where I regularly stop for a break. You are
always sitting in the sun and you have
a magnificent view of a mighty oak tree.
It is surprisingly quiet: a mini-escape in
the middle of town.'

RESTAURANTS

» **De Mangerie**, Oude Burg 20, tel.
+32 (0)50 33 93 36, www.mangerie.
com, closed on Saturday morning,
Sunday, Monday and public holidays
'Chef Kristof Deprez's dishes pay subtle
tribute to both Far Eastern and South
American cuisine, but without ever aban-
doning his Belgian roots. The result of this

melting pot of cooking ideas is an innovative mix of the very best flavours the world
has to offer. Some of the dishes are available in meatless or fishless versions. Inventive, but never far-fetched.'

» **Quatre Mains**, Philipstockstraat 8, tel. +32 (0)50 33 56 50, www.4mains.com,
closed on Sunday and Monday
'The food here is really great and you can decide the size of your own portions. From
tapas right through to your main course and dessert. And the couple that run the
place, Leen and Olivier, are just as fantastic as the food they serve.'

» **Tom's Diner**, West-Gistelhof 23, tel. +32 (0)50 33 33 82,
www.tomsdiner.be, closed on Sunday and Monday

'Although this restaurant was recently renovated by a famous interior designer, it still has a delightfully casual atmosphere. Heart-warming. Here you can eat Belgian dishes with an international twist, but without paying a fortune.'

» **Merveilleux**, Muntpoort 8, tel. +32 (0)50 61 02 09, www.merveilleux.eu,
closed on Sunday and public holidays

'A hidden jewel, where you can go for a slice of cake, a special tea, a deliciously aromatic coffee or a surprising lunch. Merveilleux does not serve standard dishes, but has a kind of 'try-it-and-see' menu, where you get several different flavours and textures on your plate. Interesting.'

» **Pane Pane**, Sint-Jakobsstraat 2, tel. +32 (0)50 49 09 54,
closed on Saturday, Sunday and public holidays

'Sometimes you don't want a full lunch but just need a budget-friendly sandwich. If so, this is the place for you. At Pane Pane your oven-fresh sandwiches are prepared right in front of your very own eyes by Gracienne and Jojo, the sweetest ladies in all Bruges.'

CAFÉS

» **Bar Salon**, Langestraat 17,
tel. +32 (0)50 33 41 13,
www.rock-fort.be, closed on Saturday, Sunday, every morning (until 12.00 noon) and every afternoon (between 2.30 p.m. and 6.30 p.m.)

'Inventive mini-dishes, original tapas and some traditional cocktail classics, all served in an adventurous contemporary interior. That is Bar Salon, a place where you can first order some excellent *jamon iberico*, followed perhaps by tuna tartare or some *pan con tomate*.'

» **Wijnbar Est**, Braambergstraat 7, tel. +32 (0)50 33 38 39 of +32 (0)478 45 05 55, www.wijnbarest.be, closed on Tuesday and Wednesday and during the day (until 4.00 p.m.)

'Noëlla and Marnix serve a fine selection of wines from around the world, by the glass or by the bottle, and they do it in a tiny – and seemingly ancient – house. Tiny? The two floors have just 10 tables in all! Even so, there is still space enough for live music on Sundays.'

» **Groot Vlaenderen**, Vlamingstraat 94, tel. +32 (0)50 68 43 56, www.grootvlaen deren.be, closed on Sunday and Monday and during the day (until 5.00 p.m.)

'A hotel bar, but without the hotel. This fancy new cocktail bar is the only place in Bruges where you can get a perfect Long Island Tea. Arne makes cocktails like the true professional he is, and is also an inspirational entrepreneur. I have great respect for his ambition.'

» **Punta Est**, Predikherenrei 1, tel. +32 (0)50 33 03 49, no closing day but closed every morning (until 10.30 a.m.)

'Undoubtedly the best sun terrace in Bruges. Away from all the tourist hustle and bustle, but still slap-bang in the middle of the city, with a really great view. The terrace is pleasantly sheltered out of the wind – but don't forget your sun-cream!'

» **De Republiek**, Sint-Jakobsstraat 36, tel. +32 (0)50 34 02 29, www. derepubliek.be, no closing day but closed every morning (until 11.00 a.m.)

'De Republiek is probably the nearest thing in Bruges to the traditional 'grand café'. In the morning you can read your paper here; later in the day you might stop by for a coffee or perhaps an aperitif in the early evening. Of course, you can always eat here. In short, a place where it is fun just to hang out. And in the summer, you can enjoy the sun in the huge interior courtyard.'

SHOPPING LIST

» **Patisserie Academie**, Academiestraat 4, tel. +32 (0)50 68 92 91, www.patisserieacademie.be, closed on Monday and Tuesday

Tom Van Loock learned the confectioner's trade at no less a place than De Karmeliet (good for 3 Michelin stars). He now runs his own patisserie, a little temple of pleasure where only perfection is good enough. The cakes look so delicious that you want to eat them right outside on the pavement.'

» **Dille & Kamille**, Simon Stevinplein 17-18, tel. +32 (0)50 34 11 80,
   www.dille-kamille.be, closed on public holidays
'A fantastic array of kitchen utensils at fantastically low prices. Here you will find everything you need to bake, roast, fry, poach and… eat! Stylish but affordable. I can never leave without buying something.'

» **De Olijfboom**, Smedenstraat 58, tel. +32 (0)50 34 16 39,
   www.deolijfboom.be, closed on Sunday and Monday
'In De Olijfboom you can find 80 different types of olive oil: 12 oils on tap, 2 *novella's* (very young oils from recently harvested olives), 20 flavoured oils (from pistachio through walnut to sesame seed), 50 kinds of vinegar and 20 types of balsamico. Add to this numerous herbs, spices and a fine selection of salts, and you can understand why it is sometimes difficult to choose what to buy.'

» **Exceller Bikes**, Philipstockstraat 43, tel. +32 (0)50 70 68 12 of +32 (0)494
   68 99 43, www.excellerbikes.com, closed on Sunday and Monday
'In this shop you don't just buy a bike. You buy a piece of biking culture. Exceller Bikes promotes a cycling life-style. In fact, the shop is more a kind of *'museum of modern biking'*. A museum full of wonderful bikes, but without all the other (often hideous) cycling paraphernalia...'

» **Oil & Vinegar**, Geldmuntstraat 11, tel. +32 (0)50 34 56 50,
   www.oilvinegar.com, closed on Sunday
'Another great foodie address, again right in the middle of town. Here you can buy all different kinds of oils, vinegars, sauces and dressings. And for a unique, personalized present, why not try one of their gift baskets: you decide exactly what goes in it. But be careful – everything in this shop is highly addictive!'

SECRET TIP

'Plan your visit to Bruges for a period when some of the year's major events are organized. This will allow you to enjoy the unique atmosphere of Bruges to the full. If your stay coincides with the Cactus Festival or the Procession of the Holy Blood, your city trip will be even more unforgettable.' *(For more information about the events in Bruges, see pages 94-97)*

Lissewege

Excursions and day trips from Bruges

Bruges' wet- and woodlands

Lissewege

Time in Lissewege seems to move just that tad slower. With its picturesque canal, whitewashed polder houses and extensive fields and meadows this polder village is a classic example of how every Flemish village once looked: lively, charming and a touch nostalgic.

Onze-Lieve-Vrouw-Bezoekingskerk (Our Lady of the Visitation Church) Lissewege

This impressive brick church was erected in an early Gothic style in the 13th century. The remarkable interior counts amongst its treasures a miraculous statue of the Virgin Mary (1625), a striking organ-case and an equally stunning rood loft and pulpit (1652). A truly great attraction is the monumental church tower. The top offers a magnificent panoramic view of the polders.

OPENING TIMES > Church: daily, 10.00 a.m. - 5.00 p.m.; during the period 1/6 until 30/9, 9.00 a.m. - 8.00 p.m. Tower: during the period 1/7 until 31/8, daily, 2.30 p.m. - 5.30 p.m.

PRICE > Church: free; tower: € 1.00; children under 12: € 0.50

INFORMATION > 'Onder de Toren', Lissewege, tel. +32 (0)50 54 45 44 (church), +32 (0)487 49 92 14 (tower), www.lissewege.be; public transport: train Bruges-Zeebrugge

Bezoekerscentrum Lissewege (Visitor Centre) Lissewege

The visitor centre traces the one thousand-year-old history of this white village by way of unique photos, maps,

models, paintings and a collection of archaeological finds from the erstwhile Cistercian Abbey of Ter Doest. At the 'Heiligenmuseum' (Museum of Saints) a unique collection of over 120 antique statues of patron saints is on display.

OPENING TIMES > During the Easter holidays (5/4 to 21/4) and during the period 15/6 to15/9: daily, 2.00 p.m.-5.30 p.m.; Whit weekend and Ascension weekend, 20/9, 21/9, 27/9 and 28/9, 2.00 p.m.-5.30 p.m.

PRICE > Museum of Saints: € 1.50; museum + coffee/tea: € 3.00; children under 12: € 1.00

INFORMATION > Oude Pastoriestraat 5, Lissewege, tel. +32 (0)50 55 29 55, www. lissewege. be; public transport: train Bruges-Zeebrugge

Abdijschuur Ter Doest (Abbey Barn) Lissewege

The commanding early Gothic abbey barn (13th century) of this former 12th century Cistercian abbey was completely restored early 2000. The dovecote (1651) and monumental gatehouse (1662) have also withstood the ravages of time brilliantly.

OPENING TIMES > Daily 10.00 a.m.-5.00 p.m.

PRICE > Free

INFORMATION > Ter Doeststraat 4, Lissewege, www.lissewege.be; public transport: train Bruges-Zeebrugge, from Lissewege station it is a 15-20 minute walk to the barn

Boudewijn Seapark Bruges

Welcome to this fun-packed family amusement park, with numerous attractions and animal spectaculars. In the recently renovated dolphinarium, the park's famous dolphins steal the show with their amazing leaps during the *Dolphin Bay Adventure*. In the sea lion theatre Captain Zeppo and sea lion Robby wait to entertain you, while in the *Nordic Lagoon* the other seals perform their crazy tricks. But there is more to the Boudewijn Seapark than its loveable sea mammals: attractions like the *Orca Ride* and the pirate ship *Sancta Maria* are guaranteed to give pleasure to the young and old alike. And to round it all off, kids can play to their heart's content in the indoor play village *Bobo's Indoor*.

OPENING TIMES > During the 'summer period' (5/4 to 28/9) the amusement park, shows and Bobo's Indoor are open: during the Easter holidays (5/4 to 21/4) and weekends in April: 10.00 a.m.-5.00 p.m.; in May and June: daily, except Wednesday, 10.00 a.m.-5.00 p.m.; July and August: daily, 10.00 a.m.-6.00 a.m.; September: only at weekends, 10.00 a.m.-6.00 p.m. During the 'winter period' (1/10 to 2/4) only Bobo's Indoor and the dolphin shows are open to the public: on Wednesday, Saturday and Sunday and during (Belgian) school holidays, 2.00-6.00 p.m.

ADDITIONAL CLOSING DATES >
1/1, 24/12, 25/12 and 31/12

PRICE > All-in ticket for the 'summer period' (park, shows and Bobo's Indoor): adults older than 12 years: € 25.00; children between 1 metre and 11 years old: € 20.00; children between 85 and 99 centimetres: € 7.00

All-in ticket for the 'winter period': adults from 12 years: € 18.50 (including drink voucher); children between 85 cm and 11 years: € 16.50; Pay& Display car park: € 7.00; Brugge City Card: € 15.00

INFORMATION AND TICKETS > A. De Baeckestraat 12, St.-Michiels, tel. +32 (0)50 38 38 38, www.boudewijnseapark.be. Tickets at the amusement park entrance or at the information office [i] 't Zand (Concertgebouw). Boudewijn Sea Park is situated just outside the city centre and is connected to the Bicycle Route Network; public transport: bus no. 7 or no. 17 - stop: 'Boudewijnpark'

Kinderboerderij (Children's Farm) De Zeven Torentjes

This 14th-century farmstead houses a merry working children's farm with a superb recreation area and a gaggle of farmyard animals. The beautifully restored dovecot and the Gothic barn are also worth a visit. Parents can wait in the cafeteria.

OPENING TIMES > Daily, from 9.00 a.m. until sunset

PRICE > Free

INFORMATION > Canadaring 41, Asse-
broek, tel. +32 (0)50 35 40 43 and +32
(0)50 37 13 04 (cafeteria); public transport: bus no. 2 - stop: Zeven Torentjes

Municipal Domains Beisbroek, Tudor and Chartreuzinnenbos

These extensive nature reserves, with a
total area of 160 hectares, ensure hours
of walking enjoyment. The vast Beisbroek municipal domain (98 hectares)
comprises woods, alleys, pastures and
heathland. A signposted trail connects
the three areas of the domain. Its nature
centre spoils nature lovers with an interactive exhibition and a children's lab.
There is also an observatory and a planetarium. You can picnic in one of the picnic areas. There is also a public observatory and planetarium.

A stone's throw away from Beisbroek is
another magnet: the Tudor Municipal
Domain. Although the Tudor-style castle
catches the eye, its ornamental garden
and herb garden are also more than
worth the while. The park itself boasts
pastures and gigantic deciduous trees.
The Chartreuzinnenbos (wood of the
Carthusian nuns; over 20 hectares) links
the 40 hectares of the Tudor Domain with
the 98 hectares of the Beisbroek Domain.

OPENING TIMES > Domains: daily; Nature
centre: during the period 1/4 until 30/11:
daily (except Saturday), 2.00 p.m.-

5.00 p.m. and on Sunday and public holidays, 2.00 p.m.-6.00 p.m.; Herb Garden: during the period 1/5 until 31/10: daily, except Saturday, 2.00 p.m.-5.00 p.m.; guided visits are possible

PRICE > Free

INFORMATION > Zeeweg 96, Sint-Andries, tel. +32 (0)50 39 09 75; public transport: bus no. 52 or no. 55 - stop: Varsenare, Zeeweg

Cozmix volkssterrenwacht (Public Observatory) Beisbroek

In the Cozmix observatory you will be able to admire the beauty of the sun, moon and planets in glorious close-up, thanks to the powerful telescope. In the planetarium more than 7,000 stars are projected onto the interior of the dome; a magnificent star-studded sky that you can even study during the day or when the weather is bad. Spectacular video images and atmospheric music take you on a journey through the mysteries of the universe: you will fly over the surface of Mars and pass through the rings of Saturn. The interactive multimedia exhibition and the artistic planet-pathway (with sculptures by Jef Claerhout) will complete your voyage of discovery into outer space.

OPENING TIMES > Wednesday and Sunday, 2.30 p.m. – 6.00 p.m., Friday, 8.00 p.m. - 10.00 p.m.; planetarium shows on Wednesday at 3.00 p.m., on Friday at 8.30 p.m., and on Sunday at 3.00 p.m. and 4.30 p.m. During (Belgian) school holidays there are extra shows on Monday, Tuesday and Thursday at 3.00 p.m. There are shows

in languages other than Dutch (one week in French, the other week in English) on Wednesday at 4.30 p.m.

ADDITIONAL CLOSING DATES > 1/1 and 25/12

PRICE > € 5.00; youngsters aged 5 to 17 years: € 4.00

INFORMATION > Zeeweg 96, Sint-Andries, tel. +32 (0)50 39 05 66, www.cozmix.be; public transport: bus no. 52 or no. 55 - stop: Varsenare, Zeeweg

Lamme Goedzak (steam wheeler) Damme

The nostalgic river boat 'Lamme Goedzak', with room for 170 passengers, sails back and forth between the Noorweegse Kaai (Norwegian Quay) in Bruges and the centre of Damme, the town of the legendary character Tijl Uilenspiegel (Owlglass), whose friend was called … Lamme Goedzak!

OPENING TIMES > During the period 1/4 until 15/10: departures from Bruges to Damme, daily at 10.00 a.m., 12.00 a.m., 2.00 p.m., 4.00 p.m. and 6.00 p.m.; departures from Damme to Bruges, daily at 9.15 a.m., 11.00 a.m., 1.00 p.m., 3.00 p.m. and 5.20 p.m.

PRICE > € 7.50 (one-way ticket) or € 10.50 (return ticket); 65+: € 7.00 (one-way ticket) or € 9.50 (return ticket); children aged 3 to 11: € 6.00 (one-way ticket) or € 8.50 (return ticket); Brugge City Card: € 8.00 (return ticket)

INFORMATION > Noorweegse Kaai 31, Brugge, tel. +32 (0)9 233 84 69, www.bootdamme-brugge.be; public transport: bus no. 4 - stop: Sasplein near the Dampoort (Damme Gate); from there it is a 5-10 minute walk to the landing stage at the Noorweegse Kaai (Norwegian Quay).

Triple Treat Quasimodo tour: the best of Belgium in one day

Take it easy on this English-language minibus tour, which takes you to, amongst others, the illustrious Tilleghem Castle and unique Neo-Gothic Loppem Castle. Included are a pleasant stroll through medieval Damme and a visit to the Gothic abbey barn of Ter Doest at Lissewege. And what would this tour be without some delicious waffles, mouth-watering chocolate and a choice selection of Belgian country ales?

OPENING TIMES > Excursions during the period 1/2 until 30/11: on Monday, Wednesday and Friday. You will be collected from your hotel or some other place of your choice in the city centre, at 9.15 a.m. and returned there at approximately 5.15 p.m. Prior reservation is necessary.

PRICE > Including lunch, admission fees and tickets: € 65.00; youngsters aged 8 to 25: € 55.00; there is an immediate € 10.00 reduction when you also book the Quasimodo WWI Flanders Fields Tour *(more info on page 155-156)*
INFORMATION > Tel. 0800 975 25 or +32 (0)50 37 04 70, www.quasimodo.be

🚌 City Tour Damme

City Tour minibuses pick you up on Bruges' market square and drop you off at Damme. Having sailed back to Bruges on Lamme Goedzak two hours later, you will be picked up by the bus at the jetty and transferred to Markt, Bruges' central square. This tour can be followed in Dutch, French, German, English, Spanish and Italian (via an audio guide per person).
OPENING TIMES > Excursions during the period 1/4 until 30/9: daily at 4.00 p.m
PRICE > Including audioguide: € 25.00; children aged 6 to 11: € 17.00
INFORMATION > Tel. +32 (0) 50 35 50 24 (Monday to Friday: 10.00 a.m.-12.00 a.m.), info@citytour.be, www.citytour.be

🏛 Uilenspiegelmuseum Damme

Would you like to know more about Tijl Uilenspiegel and his pranks and tomfoolery? And would you like to meet his clones from all over the world and understand the cultural-historical context of this capricious figure? Then Damme is your destination. Here you will not only shake hands with the famous Flemish Uilenspiegel from the 19th century, but also with his 16th-century German colleague and his various 20th-century brothers.
OPENING TIMES > During the period 1/4 until 30/9: Monday to Friday, 9.00 a.m.-6.00 p.m.; weekends and public holidays 10.00 a.m.-12.00 a.m. and 2.00 p.m.-6.00 p.m.; during the period 1/10 until 31/3: Monday to Friday, 9.00 a.m.-12.00 a.m. and 1.00 p.m.-5.00 p.m.; weekends and public holidays 2.00 p.m.-5.00 p.m.
ADDITIONAL CLOSING DATES > 1/1 and 25/12
PRICE > € 2.50; students under 27: € 1.50; Brugge City Card: € 1.50; family ticket (2 adults and children under 18): € 5.00
INFORMATION > Jacob van Maerlantstraat 3, Damme, tel. +32 (0)50 28 86 10, www.toerismedamme.be; public trans-

port: bus no. 43 - bus stop: Damme, main square or the combination of bus no. 4 - bus stop: Koolkerke 'De Ketel', followed by bell-bus no. 49 - bus stop: Damme, main square (please note: the bell-bus must be reserved by phone at least 2 hours in advance)

🛏️ Mu.ZEE
Permekemuseum Jabbeke

Constant Permeke, the most famous Flemish expressionist painter, lived and worked in Jabbeke for more than twenty years. His abode was the The Four Winds, a striking villa commissioned by the artist himself and built, for its time, in an extremely modern design. Today it is the location of the Permeke Museum, where the visitor can wander around the artist's living quarters as well as his garden and former studios. It is without a doubt the place par excellence to admire Permeke's collection of his spellbinding works in total peace and quiet.

OPENING TIMES > Tuesday to Sunday: 10.00 a.m.-12.30 a.m. and 1.30 p.m.-5.30 p.m. (till 6.00 p.m. during the period 1/4 until 30/9)

ADDITIONAL CLOSING DATES > 1/1 and 25/12

PRICE > € 3.00; 55+: € 2.50; youngsters aged 13 to 26: € 1.00; children under 13: free; Brugge City Card: € 2.25

INFORMATION > Gistelsteenweg 341, Jabbeke, tel. +32 (0)59 50 81 18, info@muzee.be, www.muzee.be; public transport: bus no. 52 or no. 53 – stop: Jabbeke Museum Permeke

🏛 Romeins Archeologisch Museum (RAM, Roman Archaeological Museum) Oudenburg

After years of trudging through mud, painstaking excavations and studies, Oudenburg today possesses a unique collection of archaeological artefacts from Roman times. The good news is that the visitor can pore over them at the modernised museum. The reconstructions, scale models, archaeological finds and computer simulations enable you to get to grips with the region's rich Roman history in a professional way. The adjacent visitor centre brings you also up to date with the Abbey of Saint Peter's, Saint Arnold and the other attractions of this region.

OPENING TIMES > During the period 29/3 until 19/10: Tuesday to Saturday, 10.00 a.m.-12.30 a.m. and 1.30 p.m.-5.30 p.m., Sunday, 2.00 p.m.-6.00 p.m.; during the period 20/10 until 28/3: Tuesday, Thursday and Friday, 10.00 a.m.-12.00 a.m., Wednesday, 10.00 a.m.-12.00 a.m. and 4.00 p.m.-6.00 p.m.

ADDITIONAL CLOSING DATES > 1/1, 2/1, 1/11, 11/11, 25/12 and 26/12

PRICE > Visitor Centre: free; museum: € 5.00; 65+: € 3.00; youngsters aged 8 to 18 and students (on display of a valid student card): € 2.00; children under 7 (accompanied by an adult): free; Brugge City Card: € 3.00

INFORMATION > Marktstraat 25, Oudenburg, tel. +32 (0)59 56 84 00, www.ram-oudenburg.be; public transport: bus no. 52 - stop: Westkerke town hall; from there, take bus no. 23 - stop: Oudenburg, Sint-Pietersstraat.

🏛 Kasteel (Castle) Wijnendale

A superb moated castle in the Torhout woods. Hours of walking pleasure guaranteed. There is more: at the castle museum the visitor makes a voyage through a thousand-year-old history by means of contemporary presentations, touch screens and a portable video guide. Witness for example Mary of Burgundy's fall from her horse and watch how King Leopold III of the Belgians surrendered to the Germans on 28 May 1940. And why don't you drop in on the former porter's lodge? It now houses a visitor's centre where you can find

everything you always wanted to know about Torhout, the Bruges wet- and woodlands, regional products, rambles, bicycle tours and so on and so forth.

OPENING TIMES > During the periods 1/4 until 30/6 and 1/9 to 30/9: Wednesday, Sunday and public holidays, 1.30 p.m-5.30p.m; during the period 1/7 until 31/8: Wednesday to Sunday and public holidays, 1.30 p.m.-5.30 p.m.

PRICE > Including video guide (palmtop, only available in Dutch): € 5.00; children aged 3 to 12: € 1.00; Brugge City Card: € 3.00

INFORMATION > Oostendestraat 390, Torhout, tel. +32 (0)50 22 07 70, www.toerismetorhout.be; public transport: train Bruges-Courtrai (Kortrijk), at the station in Torhout, take bus no. 51 or no. 64 - stop: Cambrinus

🎫 Museum Torhouts Aardewerk (Torhout Pottery Museum) Torhout

Pottery from Torhout used to be exported throughout the Western world until the Second World War. Unique pottery creations from the 16th to the 20th-century highlight the rich tradition of this al-most lost artistic craft. A splendid illustration of typical Flemish folk art influenced by Art Deco and Art Nouveau amongst others.

OPENING TIMES > During the period 15/6 until 15/9: daily (including public holidays), 9.30 a.m-12.30 p.m. and 1.30 p.m.-5.30 p.m.; during the period 16/9 until 14/6: Tuesday to Friday, 9.30 a.m-12.30 p.m. and 1.30 p.m.-5.00 p.m. and Monday, 1.30 p.m.-5.00 p.m.

ADDITIONAL CLOSING DATES > 1/1 to 5/1, 21/4, 1/5, 29/5, 9/6, 1/11, 11/11 and 25/12 to 31/12

PRICE > € 1.50, children aged 3 to 12: € 0.50; Brugge City Card: € 1.00

INFORMATION > Ravenhofstraat 5, Torhout, tel. +32 (0)50 22 07 70, www.toerismetorhout.be; public transport: train Bruges-Courtrai (Kortrijk)

A trip to the seaside

Zeebrugge

Zeebrugge is much more than a sea-port of stature. It is also a pleasant sea-side resort with an extensive beach, bathing in an informal holiday atmos-phere and boasting a fashionable mari-na as well as authentic fishermen's dis-tricts with genuine fishermen's pubs. In short, the entire world has a rendez-vous in Zeebrugge. In addition, the town is both on the Coastal Walking & Bicycle Route that connects all Flemish seaside resorts and the Bruges' wet-and woodlands Bicycle Route Network.

⛴ Port Cruise Zeebrugge

The port cruise departs from the old fishing port on board of the Zephira, a passenger ship, and sails past the naval base, the Pierre Vandamme Lock (one of the largest in the world), the LNG ter-minal, the wind farm park, Stern Island and the cruise ships and dredgers. All the time gigantic container ships are being loaded and unloaded along the

quays. Via the brand-new audio-visual guide on board you will be given infor-mation in the language of your choice about everything you see and hear during the trip. An experience that offers a unique insight into the port and its manifold activities.

OPENING TIMES > During the period 1/4 until 14/10: weekends and public holidays at 2.00 p.m.; during the period 1/7 until 31/8, daily at 2.00 p.m. and 4.00 p.m; dur-ing the period 1/8 until 17/8: daily extra round trip at 11.00 a.m.

PRICE > € 9.50; 60+: € 9.00; children aged 3 to 11: € 7.00; Brugge City Card: € 7.00

INFORMATION > Embarkation at Jacques Brelsteiger, Tijdokstraat (Old Fishing Port), Zeebrugge, tel. 32 (0)59 70 62 94, www.franlis.be; public transport: train Bruges-Zeebrugge, from the station Zee-brugge-Dorp: about 15 to 20 minutes on foot or from the station Zeebrugge-Strand: coast tram (direction: Knokke), to tram stop: Zeebrugge-Kerk (church)

The Beach at Zeebrugge

In winter this is the place par excellence to get a breath of fresh air. In summer the townspeople of Bruges flock to this wide and safe sandy strip to sunbathe, swim and potter about. You can stroll along the wide promenade of the kilometre-long Saint George's Day Walk. Amongst other things, you will pass the western break-

water and can stop at the two large viewing platforms, which offer fine vistas over the beach. The summer train station is right next to the beach, so that you can take the train almost to the waterside!

🏛 Seafront Zeebrugge

This maritime theme park in the unique setting of the old Fish Market will reveal to you all the secrets of the sea. Learn about the Belgian fishing industry, in part through the brand-new interactive expo 'Fish from board to plate', and explore the exciting world of the Port of Zeebrugge, one of Europe's busiest harbours. Dream of holidays past and future

as you discover the story of coastal tourism and admire the rich collection of miniature and North Sea shells. The more adventurous can pretend that they are the captain of the West-Hinder light ship or a sailor on the Russian submarine Foxtrot. Children can enjoy themselves on Pirate Island or in the ball-bath.

OPENING TIMES > Daily, 10.00 a.m.-5.00 p.m. (during the period 1/7 until 31/8, until 6.00 p.m.); amended opening hours during the winter; please consult the website.

ADDITIONAL CLOSING DATES > 1/1, 25/12; for the annual closure period, please consult the website

PRICE > € 12.50; 60+ and students (on display of student card): € 11.00; children under 13: € 9.00; children up to 1 metre (accompanied by parent): free; Brugge City Card: € 8.50

INFORMATION > Vismijnstraat 7, Zeebrugge, tel. +32 (0)50 55 14 15, www.seafront.be; public transport: train Bruges-Zeebrugge, from the station Zeebrugge-Dorp or Zeebrugge-Strand: coastal tram, (direction: Knokke) - stop: Kerk (Church)

🏛 Mu.ZEE Ostend

Mu.ZEE, which houses a unique collection of Belgian art from 1830 onwards, is undoubtedly one of the jewels in the Flemish museum crown: work by James Ensor, Léon Spilliaert, Constant Permeke, Jean Brusselmans, Raoul de Keyzer, Roger Raveel, Panamarenko, Luc Tuymans and many more is permanently

on view. The children's section allows your offspring to have a go at art in a playful way. It's child's play, as a matter of fact! And why not drop in on one of the great, high-profiled exhibitions? I bet you won't know where to look first!

OPENING TIMES > Tuesday to Sunday: 10.00 a.m.-6.00 p.m.

ADDITIONAL CLOSING DATES > 1/1 and 25/12

PRICE > Permanent collection: € 5.00; 55+: € 4.00; youngsters aged 13 to 26: € 1.00; children under 13: free; entrance fees are increased for temporary exhibitions; Brugge City Card: € 3.75 (permanent collection)

INFORMATION > Romestraat 11, Oostende, tel. +32 (0)59 50 81 18, www. muzee.be; public transport: train Bruges-Ostend, from the station in Ostend: bus no. 6 – stop: Sint-Jozefskerk (Saint John's church)

Mu.ZEE Ensorhuis (Ensorhouse) Ostend

Oostende is your destination if you want to wander through the mind of James Ensor (1860-1949). This house was indeed the operating base of the world-famous painter from 1917 onwards. The seashell and souvenir shop of his aunt and uncle on the ground floor has been preserved in its original state. The first floor is occupied by the Blue Salon, where Ensor lived and worked. On the first floor landing so called 'case-file' exhibitions are regularly held. But people hoping to see real works by the master will be disappointed: this small museum only contains reproductions. Even so, the Ensor House offers a fascinating journey back into the world of the early 20th century – and into the mind of a truly great artist.

OPENING TIMES > Wednesday to Monday: 10.00 a.m.-12.00 a.m. and 2.00 p.m.-5.00 p.m.

ADDITIONAL CLOSING DATES > 1/1 and 25/12

PRICE > € 2.00; 55+ and youngsters aged 13 to 26: € 1.00; children under 13: free; Brugge City Card: € 1.50

INFORMATION > Vlaanderenstraat 27, Oostende, tel. +32 (0)59 50 81 18, www.muzee.be; public transport: train Bruges-Ostend, from the station in Ostend bus no. 1- stop: Vlaanderenstraat or coastal tram (direction De Panne) – stop: Marie-Joséplein

Battlefields: Flanders and the Great War

Various day trips are organized from Bruges to the Westhoek. Prior reservation is necessary.

Quasimodo WWI Flanders Fields Tour

A guide from Quasimodo takes you on a personal and memorable minibus trip to Passendale, Hill 60, Messines Ridge, the private museum Hooge Crater in Zillebeke, several Commonwealth and German cemeteries, trenches and bunkers, the Menin Gate and numerous Australian, New Zealand, Canadian, British and Irish monuments. In short, all the highlights! The stories told by the Quasimodo guides allow you to visualize the reality of four terrible years of war in the Ieper Salient.

LANGUAGE > Explanation in English

MEETING POINT > You will be collected from your hotel or some other place of your choice in the city centre.

Departure: 9.00 a.m. Return 5.30 p.m.

OPENING TIMES > Excursions are conducted from Tuesday to Sunday in the period 1/2 to 31/12

PRICE > Including lunch and ticket Hooge Crater Museum: € 65.00; youngsters aged 8 to 25 years: € 55.00; there is an immediate € 10.00 reduction when you also book the Triple Treat Quasimodo tour: the best of Belgium in one day *(more info on pages 147-148)*

INFORMATION AND RESERVATIONS > Tel. 0800 975 25 or +32 (0)50 37 04 70, www.quasimodo.be. Tickets are also available from the info offices  on 't Zand (Concert Hall) and the Market Square (Historium)

In Flanders Fields tour

This bus tour will take you to numerous sites of interest related to the war of 1914-1918. With expert guides, you will visit the *Grieving Parents* by Käthe Kollwitz in Vladslo, the trenches along the River IJzer, the tunnels of Hill 60, the Peace Mill in Klerken and various military cemeteries in Houthulst, Poelkapelle, Boezinge and Passendale (Tyne Cot Cemetery). The day is rounded off with a visit to the In Flanders Fields Museum in Ieper and the Last Post ceremony at the Menin Gate.

LANGUAGE > Explanation in English, German and Dutch

MEETING POINT > You are collected from your hotel. Departure: 9.45 a.m. Return: 9.30 p.m.

OPENING TIMES > Every Thursday and Sunday during the period 6/4 until 26/10 and also on 8/11 and 11/11. During the period 12/7 until 14/9 there is an additional tour on Saturday

PRICE > Including lunch and ticket to the In Flanders Fields Museum: € 75.00; 65+ and students aged 26 years or less: € 69.00; children 4 to 12 years: € 39.00

INFORMATION AND RESERVATIONS > Tel. +32 (0)2 513 77 44,

www.brugge-city-tours.be , www.tickets brugge.be. Tickets are also available from the info offices [i] on 't Zand (Concert Hall) and the Market Square (Historium)

Flanders Fields Battlefield Daytours

Discover the most popular tourist attractions of the Westhoek and the Great War. You visit the German cemetery at Langemark, Tyne Cot Cemetery in Passendale, the Memorial Museum Passchendaele 1917, where you can enjoy a dugout-tunnel experience, the Menin Gate, the city of Ypres with its magnificent Cloth Hall and the not-to-be-missed In Flanders Fields Museum. The tour continues to Hill 60, Hill 62 (craters and bunkers), Heuvelland and Kemmel Hill, Messines Ridge, the mine craters of 1917, trenches and various other war monuments.

LANGUAGE > Explanation in English, French and Dutch

MEETING POINT > You are collected from your hotel. Departure: 8.45 a.m. Return: 5.15 p.m.

OPEN > Excursions from Tuesday to Sunday. No excursions during the period 13/1 to 31/1

PRICE > Including lunch, a local beer and a ticket to the In Flanders Fields Museum: € 70.00; students 18 to 26 years: € 67.00; youngsters aged 10 to 17: € 65.00

ON REQUEST > Tailor-made excursions (e.g. France). Short evening trip to the Last Post ceremony at the Menin Gate in Ypres. Departure: 6.15 p.m. Return: 9.15 p.m. Price: € 40.00

INFORMATION AND RESERVATIONS >
Tel. 0800 99 133 of +32 (0)50 34 60 60,
www.visitbruges.org

Great War Battlefields Tour

Make your acquaintance with all the most
important places on the front of the First
World War. With an experienced guide
you will explore the Trench of Death in
Dixmude (only from 1/4/2014 on) and other trenches, such as Hill 60 in Zillebeke.
The bus trip will also take you to the Canadian Memorial in Langemark-Poelkapelle,
the impressive cemeteries in Boezinge
and Tyne Cot Cemetery in Passendale. In
Ypres you will visit the In Flanders Fields
Museum and can discover the rest of this
historic front town at your own pace. You
will end the day by attending the Last
Post ceremony.

LANGUAGE > Explanation in English. In-
formation available in Dutch and French
MEETING POINT > Bargeplein (city map,
E13), under the red awning.
Departure: 9.00 a.m. Return: 9.30 p.m.
OPEN > Every Tuesday, Thursday and
Saturday during the period 1/3 until 31/12.
PRICE > Including lunch (with 2 drinks),
a local beer and a ticket to the In Flanders
Fields Museum : € 69.00; children under
13 years: € 39.00

INFORMATION AND RESERVATIONS > Tel.
0800 14 180, www.greatwarbattlefields
tour.com, www.ticketsbrugge.be.
Tickets are also available from the info offices **i** on 't Zand (Concert Hall) and
the Market Square (Historium)

★ In Flanders Fields Museum Ypres

Welcome to this recently updated and
highly interactive museum, which offers
a fascinating and memorable interpreta-
tion of the events of the Great War. This is
no dry summary of facts and figures, but
a truly participative experience that uses
modern techniques, sound effects and
authentic film images to retell the history
of the war in a manner that will leave no
one unmoved. It is almost as if you are
standing in the trenches yourself or
watching the city of Ieper being de-
stroyed with your very own eyes. Every
visitor is given a personalised poppy arm-
band, which allows you to choose your
own preferred language and also gives
access the personal histories of four par-
ticipants in the war, whose stories are
then followed throughout the museum
trajectory. In short, this is a museum that
you must experience before you can actually believe it! Until 30/6/2014, one
part of the major double exhibition organized with the Museum Dr. Guislain
in Ghent - 'War and Trauma: medical
care during the First World War' – will
be held here.

OPENING TIMES > During the period 1/4 until 15/11: daily from 10.00 a.m.-6.00 p.m. (last admission: 5.00 p.m.); during the period 16/11 until 31/3: Tuesday to Sunday, from 10.00 a.m.-5.00 p.m. (last admission: 4.00 p.m.).

ADDITIONAL CLOSING DATES > 6/1 to 20/1

PRICE > € 9.00; youngsters aged 19 to 25: € 5.00; youngsters aged 7 to 18: € 4.00; children under 7: free; Brugge City Card: € 6.50; family card (2 adults and max. 3 children): € 20.00

INFORMATION > Grote Markt 34, Ieper, tel. +32 (0)57 23 92 20, www.inflandersfields. be; public transport: train Bruges-Ypres, from the station of Ypres: bus no. 1 or no. 95 – stop: Markt (market place of Ypres)

🇨 Canada-Poland War Museum Adegem

For anyone who wants to get an idea of what happened in Flanders during the Second World War, a visit to the double Canada-Poland War Museum is a 'must'. In the Canada War Museum, life-size reconstructions of (amongst other actions) the Battle of the Scheldt, accompanied by a wide range of photographs, weapons, communication equipment and uniforms, give some idea of what life at the front was really like. For children, in the Poland War Museum they can follow the 'Second World War in Miniature', in which all the major battles are reconstructed at children's height in a scale of 1/35. In both museums children can take part in a fascinating photographic search

game. And to recover from the misery of war, you can also make a (guided only) walk in four different themed gardens: the romantic English garden, the formal French garden, the Japanese meditation garden and the exotic garden.

OPENING TIMES > Both museums: during the period 1/4 until 30/9: Wednesday to Sunday, 10.00 a.m. - 6.00 p.m.; during the period 1/10 until 31/3: Wednesday to Friday, 12.00 noon - 6.00 p.m. and in the weekends, 10.00 a.m. - 6.00 p.m. The gardens: during the period 1/4 until 30/9: Wednesday to Sunday, 1.00 p.m. - 6.00 p.m. (last guided tour starts at 4.45 p.m.)

ADDITIONAL CLOSING DATES > 1/1; annual closing: one week in October (please consult the website)

PRICE > 1 museum or gardens: € 5.00, children under 7 years: free; 2 museums: € 8.00; 2 museums and gardens: € 12.00; Brugge City Card: € 4.00 (for 1 museum), incl. postcard

INFORMATION > Heulendonk 21, Adegem, tel. +32 (0)50 71 06 66, www.canadapolandmuseum.be; public transport: bus no. 58 or no. 58S, from the centre of Adegem; bell-bus 185 (must be reserved at least 2 hours in advance) - stop: Canadees Museum (Canadian Museum)

WORLD WAR I REVISITED

In the course of 2014, there will be numerous events relating to the First World War on the Bruges cultural agenda. You can find more information and a full summary on www.brugge.be.

Other places of interest

♜ Centrum Ronde van Vlaanderen (Tour of Flanders Centre) Oudenaarde

The multi-medial Tour of Flanders Centre, in the heart of the Flemish Ardennes, is a multi-media museum with many different facets – all of them interesting! There is an interactive experience museum, an exhibition area, a film auditorium and the fun 'Tour Shop'. Last but definitely not least, there is also the Bikers Brasserie! The museum leads visitors through the history and traditions of Flanders' greatest cycling race, which is burnt into the soul of the Flemish people. Thanks to the use of multi-media magic, you can actually take part in the race yourself. Test out Tom Boonen's bike, specially designed to cope with the race's cobbled stretches, or sweat your way to the top of the Oude Kwaremont hill in the wheel of Peter Van Petegem. And once you have crossed the finishing line, mount the po-dium as winner of 'Flanders' Finest'. The friendly and helpful staff at the entrance desk will tell you everything you want to know about other tourist attractions and cycling routes in the Flemish Ardennes. Tired cyclists can even take a refreshing shower here if they want to!

OPENING TIMES > Tuesday to Sunday: 10.00 a.m.-6.00 p.m.

ADDITIONAL CLOSING DATES > 1/1, 6/1 to 27/1 and 25/12

PRICE > € 8.00; 60+ € 6.00; students and children under 15: € 4.00; family ticket (2 adults and 4 children max.): € 17.50; audioguide: € 1.00; Brugge City Card: € 6.00

INFORMATION > Markt 43, Oudenaarde, tel. +32 (0)55 33 99 33, www.crvv.be, public transport: train Bruges-Oudenaarde, from the station of Oudenaarde: bus no. 41 or no. 62 – stop: Oudenaarde Markt (market place)

Index of street names